Statistics   1960   1970

	1960	1970
Population of the United States	179.3 million	203.3 million
Number of states in the United States	50	50
Population by race:		
White	158.8 million	178.1 million
Black	18.9 million	22.6 million
Other	1.6 million	2.5 million
Population by sex:		
Male	88.3 million	98.9 million
Female	91.0 million	104.3 million
Population per square mile	50.6	57.5
Life expectancy:		
Male	66.6	67.1
Female	73.1	74.8
Number of live births	4.2 million	3.7 million
Number of radio stations:		
AM	3,483	4,288
FM	906	2,542
Number of radios per household	3.7	5.1
Number of households with television sets	45.7 million	59.5 million
Number of households with color television sets	.3 million	20.9 million
Unemployment rate	5.5%	4.9%
Median family income	$5,835	$10,236
Number of electrical engineers	188,000	286,000
Number of farm owners or tenants	2.5 million	1.2 million
Number of white collar workers	7.0 million	11.5 million
Number of junior colleges	508	886
Number of college graduates	392,440	827,234
Passenger cars registered	61,671	89,280
Gasoline consumed in gallons	41.1 million	65.7 million
Prices:		
dozen eggs	58¢	61¢
quart of milk	26¢	33¢
loaf of bread	20¢	24¢
pound of butter	75¢	87¢
pound of coffee	75¢	91¢
dozen oranges	75¢	86¢

OUR CENTURY

For a free color catalog describing Gareth Stevens's list of high-quality children's books, call 1-800-341-3569 (USA) or 1-800-461-9120 (Canada).

ISBN 0-8368-1038-4

This North American edition published by
Gareth Stevens Publishing
1555 North RiverCenter Drive, Suite 201
Milwaukee, Wisconsin 53212, USA

This edition first published in 1993 by Gareth Stevens, Inc. Originally published in 1989 by Fearon Education, 500 Harbor Boulevard, Belmont, California, 94002, with © 1989 by Fearon Education. End matter © 1993 by Gareth Stevens, Inc.

Printed in the United States of America

1 2 3 4 5 6 7 8 9 98 97 96 95 94 93

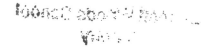

Photographs: Cover (Helicopter, President Kennedy, Sandy Koufax, the Beatles) and pp. 4-7, 9-15, 18, 20, 22-33, 36, 38-47, 50-52, 53 (top), 54-57: UPI/Bettmann Newsphotos; Cover (*New York Times* front page, Martin Luther King) and pp. 7, 16, 17, 19, 35, 37, 48, 49, 53: The Bettmann Archive; pp. 49, 52: UPI/Bettmann Archive; p. 58: Springer/Bettmann Film Archive. Advertisements inside front cover: The D'Arcy Collection, University of Illinois at Urbana-Champaign.

1960–1970

Gareth Stevens Publishing
MILWAUKEE

Flower Power

The Decade of the Hippie

If you were freethinking, or revolutionary-minded, or a nonconventional young person in the 1960s, you were probably a hippie. Hippies made up one of the biggest social protest movements of the decade. They thought there was something basically wrong with society. They rejected almost everything about traditional society.

Many hippies were college students or even graduates. Most were white, under 25 years old, and came from well-to-do, middle-class families. But they blamed "western values" and America for most of the world's problems.

The hippies rejected many traditional ideas. They felt that their parents wanted them to just get jobs, get married, and make money. Hippies called that joining the "establishment." And they were very much antiestablishment.

Instead, hippies wanted to express their individuality. It was called "doing your own thing."

If they worked at all, they worked just enough to make a living and to support other people they lived with. They didn't care about getting ahead the way their parents did.

Many hippies wanted to get "back to nature." Some left the cities to live out in the country. They didn't like using modern machines. So they learned how to do many things the old-fashioned way—by hand.

Two "flower children" at the San Francisco "Be-in" in Golden Gate Park, January 1967.

Many hippies learned to grow their own food and to make their own jewelry. They learned to hand tool leather, and to make their own clothes.

Hippies thought that their parent's generation was self-centered. They said that older people didn't care about the problems of others. At least not enough to help them with their problems. People over the age of 30 were simply not to be trusted.

The hippie movement was closely tied to the antiwar movement. They believed in peace and love. One of their slogans was: "Make love, not war."

They wore symbols of peace around their necks and sewed them to their clothes. And sometimes they carried peace signs. At this time, most males between 18 and 30 could be drafted to fight in Vietnam. Many people in this age group were against the United States' presence there.

A Drug Culture

One of the symbols of peace and love was the flower. Hippies wore flowers in their hair. And they talked about "flower power." Many people called them "flower children."

The hippies were also closely tied to drinking and drugs. Many of them smoked marijuana. And many took psychedelic drugs. Such drugs were supposed to expand the mind. One of the most widely used drugs was LSD, also called "acid."

The experience of taking LSD helped create a special type of music, called "acid rock." Drugs also influenced art and fashion. The hippie movement was associated with light shows. In these shows, colorful lights were projected on walls while music was played.

Psychologist Timothy Leary and novelist Ken Kesey were hippie spokesmen. Leary urged his followers to take drugs and to drop out of, or leave, conventional society.

But many people had "bad trips." When they took LSD or other

San Francisco's Haight-Ashbury district was considered the birthplace of the hippie movement. For some flower "children," age was obviously only a state of mind.

drugs they saw things that frightened them. Some had frightening flashbacks for a long time. Some lost touch with reality. Some, for example, leapt off buildings because they believed that they could fly.

The hippie movement peaked in 1967. That year, the hippies held a "Summer of Love." By then, San Francisco had become the hippie capital of America. Thousands of hippies flocked there that summer. They came for the "love experience."

Those who couldn't go to San Francisco, had "love-ins" in other cities. People gathered in parks to sing songs. They also took drugs and danced to rock music.

But the "Summer of Love" was a unique experience. By the end of the decade, the hippie movement was beginning to fade. But for nearly ten years, "flower power," "love beads," and "do your own thing," had been the "in thing" for millions of young Americans. ∎

Vietnam— The First "Television War"

Some called the Vietnam War the "television war." For the first time in history, people could view war at the moment it was happening.

In the past, wartime governments had always tried to control the news. Usually, they succeeded. They could describe battles any way they wanted to. They could hold back bad news. But a change came during the 1960s.

In 1965 there was a revolt in the Dominican Republic. Military men there were trying to overthrow the government. Then, President Lyndon Johnson sent the U.S. Marines there. Their purpose, he said, was to protect American citizens. But television reports showed that the Marines were helping to overthrow the government.

For the first time people could see the truth with their own eyes. The television cameras clearly disproved the government's official statements. This on-the-spot coverage of political events was upsetting to the government. In the next few years television reports on the Vietnam War would be even more upsetting.

During the Korean War, battle footage was also shown on televison. But it was days—often weeks—old before anybody saw it. And much of the film was supplied by the American government.

In March 1965 American Marines landed in Vietnam. The television crews were right there with them. Now, the networks were supplying the footage. The day's events were often shown that same night on American television. The government could no longer control what the public saw and heard.

Much of the film footage from Vietnam was like that from Korea. But there was something new in the firsthand look at war.

In August 1965, CBS showed U.S. troops in Cam Ne. This village supposedly supported the enemy Vietcong. The television cameras recorded American troops burning huts. They set fire to the straw roofs with cigarette lighters, as villagers stood by in tears, begging them to stop.

Americans had to stop and think about what they were seeing. Cam Ne may indeed have been supporting the Vietcong. Still, what Americans saw on their television sets was that Americans were destroying Vietnam. A mighty mechanized country was waging war against peasants.

As the war dragged on, more and more Americans decided that the war was a bad idea. Much of the war resistance came from what people saw on television. American troops seemed to be caught up in pointless fighting.

The war resistance itself was shown on television. The government couldn't deny that the peace movement was powerful. In their own living rooms, Americans saw huge peace demonstrations.

Early in 1968 the highly respected television newsman Walter Cronkite went to Vietnam. When he returned, his report was discouraging. He said that America might not be able to win the war. A high percentage of the viewing public believed him.

Shortly after that, President Johnson decided not to seek reelection. The main reason was that his Vietnam policy was tearing America apart. Many thought that Cronkite's report had greatly influenced the president's decision.

It looked like the turning point of a war had come not on the battlefield, but on television. ∎

A U.S. Marine looks around at the ruins in the city of Hue. Scenes such as this one were shown almost nightly on television during the sixties. They gave viewers a firsthand look at the horrors of war.

Fashion

Skirts Get Short, Hair Gets Long

There is a rule of thumb in fashion. When times are good, skirts get shorter. In the '60s the rule proved true. Business boomed, unemployment was low, and skirts got shorter.

There had never been anything like it. The new miniskirts rose a full three inches above the knee!

Not everyone liked the "minis." Many mothers refused to let their daughters expose so much of themselves. Even some fashion designers thought the style was extreme and unattractive.

Knee-high boots became very popular at the same time. But they were't tall enough. They didn't close the gap between boot and hem.

Men weren't left out of the '60s fashion scene either. Along with music, the British invasion brought Americans a new hair style—long hair for men. As the decade went on,

women's skirts got even shorter. And men's hair got even longer.

Pants changed, too. Both men and women started to wear pants that flared out around the bottom. They were called bell bottoms.

The fashions of the '60s were treated like many other things during the decade. They had their strong supporters—and they had a whole lot of people who didn't like, or understand, anything about them. ∎

"Mini" was the word for nearly everywhere including England (upper left), Denmark (upper right), and the United States (center).

U-2 Incident Heats Up Cold War

Soviets Shoot Down American Spy Plane

Francis Gary Powers kept glancing at the altitude gauge of his aircraft. It was going around very fast. It could only mean that his airplane was losing altitude. He had to think of some way to get out of it—in a few moments it would crash.

Powers didn't know yet that his airplane had been hit by a Russian rocket. And he didn't know that he was about to make history. His fateful flight would later become known as "the U-2 Incident."

Early in the morning on May 1, 1960, Powers had taken off in his U-2, a very high-flying aircraft. He had started his journey at an air base in Turkey near the Russian border. He had been ordered to fly across the Soviet Union and land at an air base in Norway. His mission was to take pictures of places the United States government wanted to know more about.

The United States had ordered Powers to keep his flight over the Soviet Union a secret. Because the Russians believe that America is a threat, no American airplanes are allowed to fly over their territory.

But U.S. president Dwight D. Eisenhower thought that it was necessary for the United States to spy on Russia. And many Americans

agreed with him. The United States believed that Russian communism was a "constant threat" to American capitalism.

So when the Russians spotted the U-2 deep inside the Soviet Union, near the city of Sverdlovsk, they shot it down. They were sure that Powers could only be a spy.

The United States tried to hide the fact that Powers was spying.

Although his plane was severely damaged, Powers was not hurt in the attack. He bailed out of the aircraft, opened his parachute, and floated safely to the ground. But as soon as he landed, he was arrested.

United States Denies Everything

The news that Powers had been shot down did not reach America until the Soviet government announced it on May 5.

At first, the United States tried to hide the fact that Powers was

spying. American officials thought he had been killed in the airplane crash. So, they denied all the Soviet accusations. U.S. officials said that the U-2 was only making weather observations and that the airplane had gone off course accidentally.

But then on May 7, Soviet premier Nikita Khrushchev announced that not only had the plane been shot down, but the pilot had been captured alive. Powers, Khrushchev said, admitted that the U-2 was a spy plane and that he was working for the Central Intelligence Agency, or CIA. The CIA is a secret government agency that gathers information about other countries.

The United States, of course, was very embarrassed. And it was forced to tell the truth about the U-2 mission.

Khrushchev was very angry over the spy episode. He said the United States wanted to wreck the Summit Conference coming up between the United States, the Soviet Union, France, and England. At the conference, the leaders of these countries planned to talk about reducing the threat of war. The meeting was set to begin on May 16 and last about two weeks.

Khrushchev also used the U-2

incident to threaten countries friendly with America. Some of them allowed the United States to base planes on their territories so that America could spy more easily on Russia. If those countries didn't stop, Khrushchev warned, Russia might attack their air bases. And, as for Powers, the Soviet Union announced that he would be tried for espionage.

Russia never did attack any air bases, but because of the U-2 incident, the Summit Conference ended in failure after only one day.

A Spy for a Spy

On August 17, 1960, Powers went on trial in Moscow for espionage. He pleaded guilty to the charges. And, over the next three days, he told the Russian court all the details of his flight. At the end, Powers was convicted and sentenced to ten years in prison.

But the story didn't quite end there. Thanks to a Russian spy, Colonel Rudolf Abel, Powers finally got out of prison and back to America.

Several years before the U-2 incident, Abel was convicted for spying against the United States. He was sentenced to 30 years in prison. But he only served five years of his sentence.

Early in 1962, the Soviet Union and the United States agreed to a "spy exchange"—Powers for Abel. The trade was made on February 10, 1962, in the German city of Berlin.

On that cold and cloudy day, the American officials brought Abel to one end of a Berlin bridge. At the other end of the bridge, Powers waited with the Russians. Both men waited for the signal that told them to start walking to the other side. When it finally came, the two men met in the center of the bridge, but no words were spoken. Then both men walked to the other side and to freedom. For Gary Powers, and for the United States, the U-2 affair had ended. ■

Francis Gary Powers (seated left in dock) at his espionage trial in Moscow, in August 1960.

The End of the Road for a Nazi War Criminal

It had taken 15 years, but finally, in May 1960, Israel captured Adolf Eichmann—the one man most responsible for carrying out Hitler's "final solution." Six million Jews had died in his death camps. Millions of other Europeans had died as well.

Most people thought Eichmann had killed himself. Many Nazi officers had committed suicide to avoid capture. Then the world found out the truth at the Nuremberg trials in 1945. Eichmann was alive! But where? No one knew.

For years many Jewish volunteers had hunted for him. And at last in 1960 their hard work paid off. They found him living in Buenos Aires, Argentina. He had changed his name to Klement. The Israelis

wanted to arrest him immediately. They had passed special laws to punish Nazi war criminals. They wanted to put him on trial in Israel. But they were faced with a problem. Since Israel had no extradition treaty with Argentina, they couldn't arrest him while he was still there. And they couldn't ask Argentina to arrest him, either. Then how could he be captured? The Israelis decided to kidnap him.

Argentina was embarrassed because Eichmann was hiding there. The government hadn't known that he was. Secretly, Argentina was pleased that Eichmann had been caught. But officially, the government had to protest the Israeli action. It said Israel had no right to kidnap Argentine citizens.

Argentina asked Israel to return Eichmann. But Israel refused. So Argentina asked the United Nations to decide what should be done. The UN ruled that Israel should apologize to Argentina. But it also ruled that Israel should be allowed to hold Eichmann for trial.

Crimes Against Humanity

Eichmann's trial was watched around the world. More than 370 news correspondents, representing 50 countries, were present. The judges came from the United States, Russia, France, and Britain. But the jury members were all Israelis.

The man in the glass booth is the notorious Nazi war criminal Adolf Eichmann. Eichmann listens as an Israeli court finds him guilty of crimes involving the mass murder of European Jews.

The former Nazi was accused of 15 crimes. He was charged with many crimes against humanity and the Jewish people. He was also accused of war crimes and of membership in a hostile organization.

Eichmann's attorney tried to defend him. He said Eichmann could not get a fair trial. Everyone in Israel had been affected by the Holocaust. So, no Israeli could judge him without prejudice. The lawyer also said that Eichmann's capture was illegal.

> ## "He was only following orders, like any other soldier."

But Israel's attorney general disagreed. No one could be neutral about genocide, he said. So the Israelis could judge Eichmann as well as anyone else. And it didn't matter how Eichmann had been captured, he went on. The UN said Eichmann should be tried.

The court ruled against the defense's arguments. Eichmann's attorney had to try something else. Eichmann could not be held responsible for his crimes, the lawyer said. He was only following orders, like any other soldier. But other Nazis had used the same argument at the Nuremberg trials. And it failed then, as it did now.

Eichmann was convicted on all but one charge. And he was sentenced to death. On May 31, 1962, he was hanged. It had taken a long time, but Hitler's "servant of death" had finally paid the penalty for his murderous crimes. ■

A symbol of anger and fear, the Berlin Wall cuts through the center of the German city. Barbed wire and steel beams help to prevent passage.

Berlin's Wall of Shame

It appeared out of nowhere, almost overnight. It was a symbol of the tension and bitterness caused by dividing a city and its citizens. The people of Berlin, Germany, called it *Schandmauer*, a wall of shame. The rest of the world simply called it the Berlin Wall.

The city of Berlin had been the center of the "cold war" between the United States and Russia for years. While the entire city was located inside Soviet-controlled East Germany, Berlin itself was a divided city. Since the end of World War II, West Berlin had been a "free" sector, its freedom guaranteed by American,

British, and French forces. East Berlin was controlled by the Soviet Union.

Over the years, the Soviets had tried to pressure the Western allies to withdraw from West Berlin. The Russians wanted to unite the entire city under East German communist rule. But for more than 16 years, the Western countries had refused to leave. West Berlin was an important symbol of freedom to the world. The Western allies did not want to lose that symbol.

In June 1961, Soviet premier Nikita Khrushchev renewed his demands that the Western nations

leave West Berlin. If they did not, he threatened to sign a separate peace treaty with East Germany. Under the treaty, East Germany would control all access routes to West Berlin. That would certainly endanger the "free" status of that sector.

U.S. president John F. Kennedy wasn't worried. He felt sure that Khrushchev didn't really want to fight over Berlin. After all, Khrushchev had threatened Berlin before—but nothing had happened.

But Kennedy didn't realize how unhappy the Soviets were with the situation in Berlin. Although the city was divided, East Berliners could ⇨

easily cross into West Berlin each day. Many of them had jobs in the Western sector and even relatives there. For many people, traveling back and forth between sectors was a part of everyday life.

East German Economy Suffers

But as tensions continued to increase between the Soviets and the United States, many East Germans went over to West Berlin—and didn't come back. They remained in the free sector for good. By midsummer 1961, 1,000 people a day were fleeing East Berlin and settling in the West.

This made things very hard in East Germany. Soon, there weren't enough doctors or factory workers. And there weren't enough farmers to grow food. So food had to be rationed. The Russians decided to stop the flow of people to the West. They were afraid the East German economy might break down.

So, the East Germans started bringing in supplies to build a wall around West Berlin. By August 12, the East Germans were ready. They held a secret meeting, and that night closed all the roads to West Berlin. They put up temporary barricades until they could build a permanent wall.

By midsummer 1961, 1,000 people a day were fleeing East Berlin and settling in the West.

The East Germans began stopping trains and cars. No one could cross the border. Russian tanks came into East Berlin. Telephone lines to West Berlin were cut.

At first, the Western powers were afraid to react. This made the West Germans angry. They wanted to stop the Russians and East Germans from closing the border.

West Berliners were especially upset. Many of them had relatives and friends in East Berlin. They were afraid they might not see each other again. So West Berliners gathered at the border crossings. They yelled at the East German guards. And they threw stones.

Many East Germans took advantage of the confusion. They escaped to West Berlin. They knew it would be much harder after the wall was finished.

France, Britain, and the United States protested the border closings. But Russia and East Germany didn't listen. They passed another new law. The new law required West Berliners to get a special permit to cross the border. And that wasn't all. Russia and East Germany also wanted to cut the number of crossing points.

The Western allies protested again. They said these rules were illegal. They brought troops up to the border. Infantry units pitched their tents near the barricades. And armored cars patrolled up and down. Ten American tanks were brought up to one of the crossing points, their cannons pointing east.

On October 27, the Russians also brought 10 tanks up to the border. They were placed just opposite the American ones. Then the Russians brought up 20 more tanks. So the United States sent in 20 more of its own.

The next day, the Russians pulled back their tanks. They backed down. The crisis was suddenly over.

But by then the Berlin Wall had been built. The Western allies weren't forced to leave West Berlin. But they did have to accept a situation they didn't like. There would continue to be two Germanies, and two Berlins, which are unlikely to be rejoined. And overshadowing the German people would be a 26-mile-long wall symbolizing the denial of freedom to an entire city. ∎

American tanks rumble up to Checkpoint Charlie on the East-West Berlin border on October 28, 1961. There they faced an equal number of Russian tanks. After 17 tense hours, the Russian tanks backed off to a side street.

The People's Pope

Angelo Roncalli reigned as Pope John XXIII for only four years and seven months. But in that short time, he initiated sweeping changes that would affect millions of people for years to come. And he became one of the most popular popes in the history of the Catholic Church.

When Cardinal Roncalli was elected pope on October 9, 1958, one of his first acts was to call an ecumenical council. It had been nearly a hundred years since such a worldwide meeting had been held. But now Pope John wanted all the bishops of the Catholic Church to meet him at the Vatican. All over the world people were surprised. The new pope was 76 years old. Nobody expected him to do anything more than carry on church tradition.

He said the Church needed *aggiornamento*, or new life. It was too old and tired. He wanted to "open the window, to let in fresh air."

Many of the Church's leaders were upset. They thought the Church was fine just as it had always been. They didn't want to make any changes. So they tried to stop the pope.

But Pope John went ahead with his plans. And finally, on October 11, 1962, he opened the first session of the ecumenical council, which had come to be known as Vatican II. It was only the second time in history that all the Church's bishops had been called together.

Pope John did more than just gather the bishops together. He even invited leaders of other churches to the Vatican Council. They were allowed to watch the meetings. And they got to meet the pope. Pope John told them he wanted to unite all of Christianity. He wanted all Christians to work together for worldwide peace.

Vatican II was big news. Reporters from all over the world came to Rome to cover the story. It was one of the most widely discussed religious events of the century.

Very Humble Beginnings

Angelo Roncalli never thought he would hold the Church's most holy office. After all, he was from a peasant family without power or connections. He was ordained a priest in Rome in 1904. Later he served in the Italian Infantry during World War I. Then he worked as a professor of theology for nine years. When he was still very young, he worked as a secretary for an unusually modern bishop. So he was exposed to new ideas even then. In the bishop's office, he also got to know many important Church leaders. Later on, these friendships became very important for his career.

Next the Church made him a diplomat and sent him to the East. For many years he worked as the pope's official representative in Bulgaria and Turkey. Most ambitious priests didn't like being sent to the East. It was too far from Rome. Such an assignment usually meant that they would be forgotten. Archbishop Roncalli had good reason to think his career would be stalled.

The Church was too old and tired, Pope John said.

But then, surprisingly, the Church made him papal nuncio to France. It was an important promotion. And at first, he thought they must have made a mistake. But, it was no mistake. His skill at dealing with people had earned him a good reputation.

The Church was very happy with the job he did in France. So in 1953, he was named a cardinal. Soon

The "Pope of the People" makes news wherever he goes. Here, on October 7, 1961, Pope John XXIII makes his way to the chapel of the new Philippine Pontifical Seminary on the outskirts of Rome.

after, he was made patriarch of Venice. Now he was sure that he would go no higher. He already held a very important job. Then in 1958 Pope Pius XII died. And the Church needed a new leader. But no one, least of all Angelo Roncalli, could have guessed that he would be elected to succeed the deceased pope. But he was.

As pope, John XXIII was different from other popes in many ways. In spite of his solemn office, he was a warm, kind man with a lively sense of humor. As the son of a humble tenant farmer, he always felt at one with the common people.

He often traveled around Rome while other popes had rarely left Vatican City. He even went to watch the 1960 Olympic Games, which were held in Rome.

When Pope John died of a stomach tumor on June 4, 1963, the whole world was saddened. More than 35,000 Romans came to hear his funeral mass.

His reign may have been very short. But no pope in modern history has ever made such an impact as Pope John XXIII. ∎

Soviet ruler Nikita Khrushchev was suddenly ousted from power in October 1964.

The Fall of a Soviet Ruler

He had ruled the Soviet Union completely since 1957. Under his reign the United States had been continually embarrassed by Soviet accomplishments in space. And America had been forced to accept a Soviet-sponsored Communist state—Cuba—only 90 miles from U.S. shores.

So in the early fall of 1964, Khrushchev seemed to be at the height of his power. Then suddenly, on October 15, he was gone. He had been ousted from his leadership post and replaced by two Communist party officials.

Although Khrushchev had tried to intimidate the West at every opportunity, in many ways, he was also popular.

Khrushchev's rise to power began when Josef Stalin died in 1953. It was then that Khrushchev began to "de-Stalinize" Russia. Stalin had ruled by fear. Even after his death, many Russians were afraid to speak against him. But Khrushchev relaxed their fears. He also began talking about the idea of "peaceful coexistence" with the West. This was a dramatic change from previous Soviet policy. In the past, the Soviets felt that Western capitalism had to be actively opposed. But the thinking behind peaceful coexistence, was that the two societies could live side by side.

Khrushchev's power had been challenged once before. In 1957, army marshal Georgi Zhukov had helped put down a rebellion against Khrushchev. And after that, he became even more powerful. To many people, it seemed that he was firmly in control. But in the early 1960s, Khrushchev began to suffer setbacks.

One failure was his country's relations with Red China. Khrushchev didn't get along with China's leader Mao Tse-tung. Mao wanted to keep the United States out of the Formosa Straits between Red China and Nationalist China. And he wanted Khrushchev to help him. But Khrushchev refused.

Together, the two nations represented most of the Communist world. But they had many other disagreements, and finally they broke off relations. At the same time, Albania, once a strong Soviet ally, also split with Moscow. It sided with Red China in the dispute.

Khrushchev also had trouble with other countries controlled by the Soviet Union. Under pressure, he allowed those countries more freedoms. But the people kept demanding even more changes. Finally, his "iron hand" policies led to troubles in Poland, Hungary, and Rumania.

One day Khrushchev was in charge . . . then suddenly he was gone.

At home Khrushchev also had problems. The party leaders were unhappy with his unsuccessful farming program. Since Russia wasn't able to grow enough food for its people, the Soviets had to depend more on the West for imported goods.

Many people in the West were surprised when Khrushchev was toppled from power. Much of his political trouble at home was never made public outside the inner Communist party circles.

One day he was in charge. The next day the announcement was made that the Central Committee had replaced Khrushchev and appointed Leonid Brezhnev as party first secretary and Alexi Kosygin as premier.

In many ways Khrushchev's removal was accomplished in the same fashion he had used to remove his chief rivals for power during the 1950s—in secret. In the Soviet Union the leaders may change, but the system for grabbing and holding power seems to basically remain the same. ∎

After Nikita Khrushchev was ousted, the new leaders of the Soviet Union were (left to right): Communist party chief Leonid Brezhnev; Soviet premier Alexei Kosygin; and Soviet president Nikolai Podgorny.

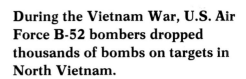

During the Vietnam War, U.S. Air Force B-52 bombers dropped thousands of bombs on targets in North Vietnam.

Escalation in Vietnam: The Road to War

It began with an attack on two U.S. naval vessels thousands of miles from home. No lives were lost, and not much damage was done. But the incident triggered the involvement of U.S. troops in the longest, bloodiest, and most controversial war in American history.

On August 2, 1964, the U.S. destroyers *Maddox* and *C. Turner Joy* were on patrol. It was their normal duty in the Gulf of Tonkin off the coast of North Vietnam. Three North Vietnamese patrol boats began pursuing the ships. Then the patrol boats launched torpedoes and the American ships fired back.

The captain of the *Maddox* asked a nearby aircraft carrier for help. Soon three jets swooped down on the North Vietnamese boats. One of the patrol boats was sunk.

In Washington, D.C., President Lyndon B. Johnson was angry about the attack. The United States claimed its ships were in international waters and were no threat to North Vietnam. So the North Vietnamese should not have attacked them.

In Hanoi, the North Vietnamese government denied making the attack. But Johnson stuck to his charge. He warned the North Vietnamese not to attack any other U.S. ships. Otherwise, he said, America would retaliate.

Two days later, the *Maddox* reported another attack. But no one on board actually saw any North Vietnamese patrol boats in the area.

That same day, August 4, Johnson publicly announced that the two attacks had occurred. He told the American people that the United States would retaliate for the attacks. The next day, two U.S. aircraft carriers launched a major air strike against North Vietnam. They bombed ships and ports along the

Gulf of Tonkin. The entire affair became known as the "Tonkin Gulf Incident."

Johnson Seeks Wider War

Before the attacks, Johnson had been thinking about expanding U.S. involvement in the conflict in Vietnam. His plan included bombing North Vietnamese cities and it called for blockading Haiphong harbor, the country's main port.

Johnson couldn't expand the U.S. role in the war unless Congress approved. And Johnson wasn't sure that he had enough support. So he hesitated for several months. When the North Vietnamese attacked the *Maddox*, Johnson decided it was time to show his plan to Congress.

Some people didn't believe the *Maddox* was attacked. They thought Johnson was using the incident as an excuse to get congressional support. When the North Vietnamese denied attacking the *Maddox*, some people believed them.

But most members of Congress believed the president. They reviewed his plan. And on August 7, 1964, all but two members voted to support it. The plan was called the "Gulf of Tonkin Resolution."

The Gulf of Tonkin Resolution was a very important document. It gave the president special powers to wage war in Vietnam. Until then, America's role in Vietnam was very limited. There were many U.S. troops in Southeast Asia, but they were only there as advisers. Their job was to teach the South Vietnamese how to fight.

After the Gulf of Tonkin Resolution was passed, however, America was slowly sucked deeper and deeper into a major war. ■

Wounded American soldiers wait for a helicopter to carry them to a hospital.

Vietnam: A Long-Term Conflict in Southeast Asia

Vietnam has been at war for a long time. The country had once been a French colony. But in the late 1940s, the Vietnamese began fighting for their independence.

The Vietnamese finally drove out the French in 1954. But the war left the country divided. In the north, the communists set up a government. The south was ruled by people friendly to the United States.

The North Vietnamese wanted to control the south. But South Vietnam wanted to be independent. So they began fighting all over again. But this time, the Vietnamese were fighting among themselves.

The United States offered help to South Vietnam. First President Eisenhower, and then President Kennedy sent military advisers to aid the South Vietnamese army. When Lyndon B. Johnson became president, there were about 16,000 American advisers in South Vietnam.

At the same time, North Vietnam was getting food and arms from the Soviet Union and China.

Then the passage of the Gulf of Tonkin Resolution allowed Johnson to escalate the war. At first, the United States focused on building an air war. Many military people wanted to bomb North Vietnam. The communists had many troops in South Vietnam. But their supplies came from the north. The military believed that the bombing would stop the flow of supplies. And that in turn would boost South Vietnam's morale.

> By 1965 the United States was bombing North Vietnam regularly.

So the United States began setting up air bases in South Vietnam and in neighboring Thailand. Thousands of planes were brought in from all over the world. And aircraft carriers were stationed off the coasts of Vietnam.

The number of air attacks increased gradually, and by February 1965, the United States was bombing North Vietnam regularly. The bombing campaign was unlike any other in U.S. history. It was directly controlled by President Johnson. In other conflicts, the air war had been directed by military men. But Johnson personally selected bombing targets in Vietnam. And he decided when they would be attacked. He also controlled the number of planes and bombs that would be used.

The bombing did very little damage to North Vietnam's war effort. But many people still thought it was a good idea. They believed it showed the North Vietnamese that the United States was prepared to help the South fight off the communists.

There was also growing pressure to send in U.S. combat troops. Because the air bases in South Vietnam had to be protected, Johnson sent a few Marines to Vietnam in March 1965. They were the first American combat troops to do more than advise the South Vietnamese. They had come to *fight* in the war.

U.S. Marines fire into a South Vietnamese village hut. It was believed to be a Vietcong headquarters from which sniper fire had come.

When they first arrived, the situation was not good. Many areas in South Vietnam were controlled by the Vietcong. These guerrilla fighters did their best to disrupt daily life in those areas. But many U.S. officials were worried about South Vietnamese morale. They were afraid that the South Vietnamese might be offended if American troops took over the war. So they wanted to limit U.S. participation. Eventually, though, they lost the debate to those who wanted to expand the war.

Throughout 1965, the United States increased its combat role in the war. In April, Johnson decided that 82,000 soldiers should be sent to Vietnam. In May, he asked Congress for more money for the military. Only ten congressmen opposed the increase.

Other countries also sent troops to help South Vietnam. Among them were Australia, Korea, and the Philippines. They supplemented the American forces there.

Still the United States had the largest commitment of troops in Asia. By the end of 1965, some 180,000 American troops had arrived in South Vietnam. And 250,000 more were on their way.

But each time the United States stepped up its efforts, so did the North Vietnamese. The battles got bloodier. The death toll climbed higher. And the pattern continued throughout 1966 and 1967.

In early 1967, about 30,000 U.S. and South Vietnamese troops defeated a large North Vietnamese and Vietcong force. The spot, just northwest of Saigon, capital of the South, was a major center of operation for the Vietcong. Later that year, in a major air battle, U.S. fliers shot down seven enemy planes. But in spite of these victories, things seemed to get worse. The war continued to rage. And more American troops were sent into battle. In January 1967, Johnson asked Congress for a tax increase to help pay for the war. In July, another

55,000 soldiers were shipped off to Vietnam.

That fall, U.S. forces fought the Battle of Dakto. It was one of the longest and bloodiest battles of the war. It lasted nearly three weeks. More than 1,455 North Vietnamese soldiers were killed. And 285 Americans died.

Back home, support for the war was beginning to wane. After the Dakto battle, the Senate Foreign Relations Committee made an important decision. It voted unanimously to cut back on the number of troops sent to Vietnam.

However, by the end of 1967 there were still 500,000 American servicemen in Vietnam. ■

Thousands of small children were victimized by war in Vietnam.

Helicopters played a major role in the U.S. military involvement in Vietnam.

Tet 1968: The War Reaches a Turning Point

Tet is Vietnam's biggest and most important holiday. In both North and South Vietnam, everyone celebrates the lunar new year.

In 1968 the Tet holiday began on January 30. During the past few years of the war, both sides had observed a cease-fire for the holiday. Therefore, many people were shocked when the North Vietnamese launched a major attack on the first day of the celebration.

It was the biggest offensive ever launched by the North Vietnamese.

The campaign began with several attacks at once. These attacks were mainly directed at large cities and district capitals in the South. Many South Vietnamese soldiers were on leave for the holiday. So they were not prepared for a strong defense against the assaults.

The battles lasted for several weeks. The North Vietnamese forces reached key targets around Saigon, including the grounds of the U.S. embassy and U.S. Army headquarters. They also captured the

important city of Hue and held it for nearly a month.

Eventually the Americans and South Vietnamese beat back the offensive. The North Vietnamese and Vietcong failed in their attempt to spur an organized revolt against the South Vietnamese government.

In addition, the North Vietnamese and Vietcong suffered heavy losses. They were forced to retreat to positions they had held before the offensive. When the U.S. and South Vietnamese forces recaptured

territory, it boosted the morale of their troops.

But back in the United States, Tet was viewed as a major defeat. Up until then, Americans believed that they were winning the war. That's what U.S. military leaders and President Johnson had been saying for months. Now, it appeared as if the war was no closer to an end than it had been back in 1965. Even many supporters of the Johnson administration began to admit that no military solution to the war was likely soon.

A survey was taken just after the offensive ended. It showed that 60 percent of the American public believed that the Tet Offensive was a defeat for the South Vietnamese forces.

The Tet campaign helped to unite various U.S. antiwar groups into a major political force. President Johnson was soon forced to stop bombing North Vietnam. And the pressure became great even within his own party. So, in March 1968, he decided not to seek renomination for another term as president.

Congress launched an investigation of the war. Many legislators began to wonder if they had been told the truth about the Tonkin Gulf

Before Tet, Americans had thought they were winning the war.

Incident. Had the president lied to them so that they would pass the resolution allowing him to escalate the war?

By the middle of 1968, debate was raging back home about the conduct of the war. But 10,000 miles from America's shores, the fighting continued—with no end in sight. ∎

The Guerrilla War of the Vietcong

In many ways, the Vietnam War was like no other war America had ever fought. It was a guerrilla war. This meant that much of the time, the enemy stayed hidden, making attacks by surprise. Often, American soldiers didn't even know who the enemy was. Innocent-looking villagers—men, women, and even children—often turned out to be Vietcong.

The Vietcong lived in South Vietnam. They were Communist guerrilla fighters from both the South and the North. They were supported by North Vietnam. They helped the North Vietnamese by attacking villages in the South. They blew up buildings and terrorized the civilians. And they kidnapped and tortured people they suspected of cooperating with the South Vietnamese government.

Many South Vietnamese helped the guerrillas by feeding them and hiding them when necessary. Some did so out of fear. Others helped because they sympathized with the Vietcong cause.

So the U.S. troops had to fight the Vietcong guerrillas. And they also had to help repel an invasion of the South by the North Vietnamese army. Many battles were fought between the U.S. and North Vietnamese soldiers. It all became very confusing. U.S. troops had a difficult time understanding the progress of the war. Even when they won a battle, they didn't seem to gain anything.

One example was the major battle fought at Apbia Mountain in May 1969. After ten days of hard fighting, U.S. troops finally captured the mountain. But many Americans were killed, as were many North and South Vietnamese. So much blood was spilled that the mountain was renamed "Hamburger Hill."

Later, American troops were ordered to abandon the hill. So the North Vietnamese recaptured it. This was hard for the U.S. troops to understand. Why should they fight for territory and then give it back to the enemy? It seemed to many American soldiers that they were fighting and dying for nothing. The result was inevitable. Morale among American troops declined sharply as the war dragged on.

Paris Peace Talks Stalled

Vietnam War Drags On and On and On . . .

When Richard M. Nixon became president, in January 1969, the United States had been involved in the Vietnam War for nearly four years. And more than 31,000 American soldiers had died in Asia.

By the beginning of Nixon's term, support for the war was nearly gone. Antiwar riots and protests had become common at home. And anti-American feelings had taken root around the world.

Still, despite all the pressure, no peaceful solution to the conflict seemed at hand.

As early as 1964, President Lyndon Johnson was looking for a way out of Vietnam. Between 1964 and 1968, there were more than 17 bombing pauses. Each one was intended to help bring peace. But each one failed to produce peace talks—and the bombing always resumed.

During the same period, the United States put forth dozens of different peace proposals. None of them were acceptable to North Vietnam.

From the beginning, the Communists wanted the United States to stop bombing North Vietnam—permanently. Only then they would agree to talk. They rejected

---

No peaceful solution to the conflict seemed at hand.

---

many U.S. peace proposals because this was not included in the plans.

In June 1967, the Hanoi govern-

Reporters look on as the Paris Peace Conference opens on May 13, 1968. The Americans and North Vietnamese argued for several weeks before they finally agreed on the shape of the conference table.

ment rejected another proposal. This time, it was because the Vietcong would not be included in any peace talks.

In March 1968, Johnson made an important televised address. He agreed to stop bombing the North. He also announced that he would send 13,500 more troops to Vietnam. And he said he would bow out of the 1968 presidential race.

A few days later, North Vietnam said it was ready to talk peace. But progress was very slow. Many of the discussions were fruitless and to some, they seemed downright silly. For more than a month, the two sides argued over the choice of the meeting site. They finally agreed on Paris, France. Then, for several weeks, they argued over the shape of the conference table. They also disagreed on the seating arrangements.

At first, the South Vietnamese and the Vietcong were not included in the talks. The South Vietnamese were worried about this. They feared the United States and North Vietnam might reach a peace settlement by themselves. And that the terms might not be favorable to South Vietnam.

Finally the North Vietnamese said they would let South Vietnam participate in the discussions if the United States agreed to allow the Vietcong a seat at the table. So the United States agreed.

Much time had already gone by. And the two sides hadn't even discussed any peace proposals yet. In fact, the talks didn't officially open until January 18, 1969. That was ten months after Hanoi had agreed to meet.

"Fight and Talk" Strategy

When the talks started, it was time for Johnson to leave office. He gave a farewell address to the nation. In the speech, he said he hoped President Nixon would be able to settle the war.

But as Nixon took over, the North Vietnamese stuck to their strategy of "fight and talk." And they

U.S. Marines dash to their bunker for cover during a Communist artillery assault at Khe Sanh.

began insisting that America withdraw its troops. Otherwise, they said there could be no settlement.

Many people were convinced that Johnson's peace strategy had been wrong. He had refused to withdraw any American troops until a peace settlement was reached.

Nixon said that America would have "peace with honor."

Now Nixon said he would withdraw troops, but first, there had to be progress made at the peace talks. He proposed to "Vietnamize" the war. That meant that American soldiers would be withdrawn gradually, and their duties would be taken over by South Vietnamese troops. America would have "peace with honor," Nixon said. And South Vietnam would defend itself.

But in February 1969, the number of American soldiers in Vietnam reached an all-time high. As

the months went on, Nixon didn't seem to be living up to his pledge.

It seemed that he really wanted the North Vietnamese to surrender. So he continued to bomb North Vietnam. And he began bombing their hide-outs in neighboring Cambodia.

But later, Nixon gave in to North Vietnamese demands. In July 1969, the first U.S. troop reductions began. The government announced plans to bring home 100,000 men by the end of the year.

In September, Nixon also decided not to draft 48,000 new men. Finally the war seemed to be slowly winding down.

Then, in December, the North Vietnamese walked out of the peace talks. They returned to the talks, shortly thereafter, but no significant progress was made.

More Americans came home. But more were also dying. By the end of the decade, more than 40,000 Americans had died. And more than 260,000 had been wounded, were missing, or had been captured.

Vietnam was already the longest war in American history. And no one yet knows when it will end. ∎

Israeli soldiers celebrate their capture of the old city of Jerusalem from the Jordanians.

And on the Seventh Day . . . Israel Rested

From the day of its birth in May 1948, the nation of Israel was threatened. Within 24 hours after it was created by an act of the United Nations, Israel was attacked by its Arab enemies—the armies of Egypt, Syria, Jordan, Lebanon, and Iraq. By the end of the year, however, the new Middle Eastern state had defeated its enemies and had driven them out of its territory.

Lasting peace was hard to obtain though. For the next 20 years or so, tensions in the region remained high. After another war between Israel and Egypt in 1956, United Nations troops had been stationed in the Sinai Peninsula. They were sent there to prevent further fighting between the countries in the area. But there were still plenty of clashes between the Israelis and their hostile Arab neighbors.

In May 1967, Egypt's president Gamal Nasser asked the UN to remove its troops from the Sinai Peninsula. The UN granted his demand. To many people this seemed to be a sign that Egypt was preparing for another war. And that Nasser didn't want the UN troops to interfere.

Later that month, Nasser made another hostile move. He closed the Gulf of Aqaba to Israeli shipping by blocking the Straits of Tiran. Now it became *clear* that Egypt was preparing for war. Shortly after that the Arab countries called up their army reserves.

Then Israel called up its own army reserves. It was obvious that war was coming—a war Israel could not afford to lose. The Arabs had lost other wars, but they kept coming back to fight again. It was a different story for Israel. If the young nation lost just one war, it would mean the end of Israel!

Israel waited for the rest of the world to do something to prevent the war. But no other countries offered help. Israel stood alone. So Israel decided to strike first!

On June 5, Israeli planes swooped in over the airfields of Egypt, Jordan, and Syria. In a few minutes, almost all of the grounded Arab airplanes were destroyed. Israel lost only 19 planes. This first day of war was a disaster for the Arabs.

The second day of the war was even worse. Part of the Egyptian army surrendered. So did the Palestinian Liberation Army. And on the third day, the Israeli navy was in control of the Straits of Tiran.

On June 8, the fourth day, Israeli troops occupied the Gaza Strip, the Sinai Peninsula, and the West Bank (Jordanian territory west of the Jordan River).

On the fifth day the Israelis reached the Suez Canal. They destroyed more than 150 Egyptian tanks in one day of fighting. And the rest of the Egyptian army retreated.

On June 10, the sixth day, the Golan Heights in Syria fell to Israel. The Syrian army was nearly destroyed. Many officers deserted. More than one third of Syria's 300 tanks were destroyed. And another 40 tanks were captured. Syria also lost 50 percent of its artillery.

The war was over. In just six short days, Israel had defeated the combined forces of the strongest Arab nations in the Middle East. The world was stunned. The Arab countries were in complete shock. The tiny nation of Israel had beaten its enemies into the ground before they even knew what hit them.

Many supporters of Israel rejoiced at its lightning-fast victory. But many other people around the world saw no real reason for joy. Another war had been fought in the Middle East. More people had been killed, more citizens were left homeless, more property was totally destroyed. And although the Arab nations had been defeated, they still vowed to destroy Israel one day. No peaceful solution to a decade-old problem seemed likely in the near future. ■

Soviets Crush a Czech Reform Movement

The people called it the "Prague Spring." It was a season of hope for millions of Czechoslovakians who yearned for freedom and a voice in their government's policies. But in the end, those hopes were crushed in the summer heat by Soviet tanks.

The government of Czechoslovakia had been Communist since the end of World War II. For 20 years the state had controlled all businesses, industry, churches, and schools. But the Communist party was unpopular with thousands and thousands of people. They wanted to be free. But many Czechs who opposed the government were imprisoned by the secret police.

In the late 1960s, Czechoslovakia suffered a sharp economic decline. Production dropped and there were shortages of food and other goods. This situation made the people even more unhappy with the party's rule. Many citizens began to call for more freedom.

Some top members of the Czech Communist party agreed with the people that change was needed. In January 1968, the party leaders removed the current Czech party chief, Antonin Novotny. They replaced him with Alexander Dubcek, one of the reform-minded members.

Throughout the spring, Dubcek's leadership introduced a series of liberal reforms. These included more freedom of the press and increased contacts with non-Communist nations. Open criticism of the party and the government was now permitted to a greater extent.

As happy as the Czechoslovakians were about the reforms, the Soviet Union was unhappy. Russia controlled the Communist party in Czechoslovakia the way it did in many other Eastern European countries. These countries made up the Warsaw Pact—a group of allied nations controlled by the Soviet Union.

The last thing Russia wanted was for one Warsaw Pact nation to "step out of line" from the others. If the Czechs were granted more freedom, then the Poles, Hungarians, Bulgarians, East Germans, and many others might demand the same.

> The last thing Russia wanted was for any Warsaw Pact nation to "step out of line."

The Dubcek reforms continued throughout the early part of the summer. And the Soviet leaders became even more concerned.

The Soviet leadership was fearful that the Czech reforms would cause other Eastern nations to push for change. So on the night of August 20, the Soviets and their Warsaw Pact allies invaded Czechoslovakia with tanks and nearly 600,000 troops.

Czech citizens quickly formed an underground. People hid radios. And they put up anti-Russian signs. They even hurled garbage at the Russian tanks. But they were no match for the Red Army.

Dubcek and his top aides were taken to Moscow by force. There the Soviets forced them to restore some of the old hard-line policies.

The Czech leaders were a defeated group when they returned home. Over the next several months many of the reformers in the Czech leadership were removed. Finally in April 1969, Dubcek himself was forced out as party first secretary.

By the end of the decade, thousands of liberal Czechoslovakian Communists had resigned or been removed from the party. The pro-Soviet leaders were firmly in control. The "breath of fresh air" brought on by the Prague spring was gone. In its place was the foul air brought on by Soviet tanks. ∎

Angry Czech citizens surround a Soviet tank in Prague during the Soviet invasion in August 1968.

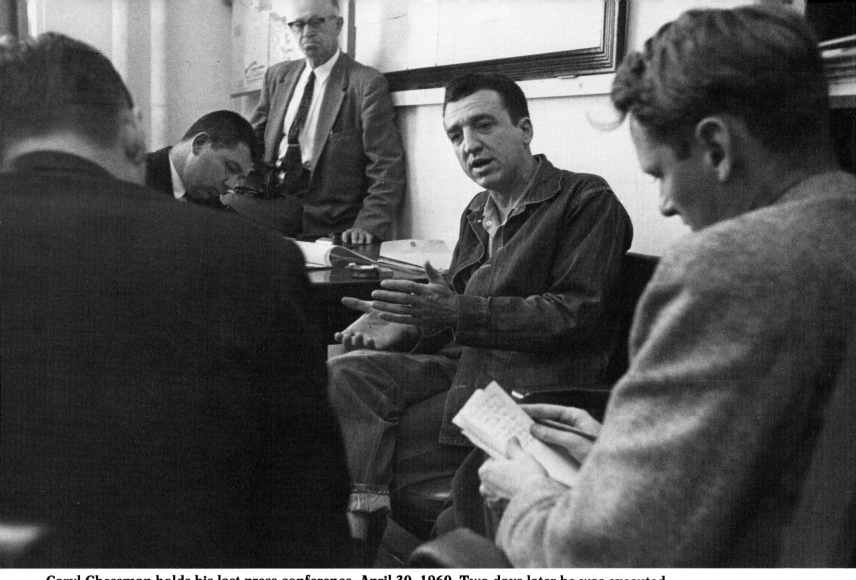

Caryl Chessman holds his last press conference, April 30, 1960. Two days later he was executed.

Caryl Chessman's Long Battle Against Death

It all began in Los Angeles, California, in 1948. The courtroom scene was grim—but not that unusual. A man named Caryl Chessman was convicted of 17 different crimes. Two of those convictions carried the death penalty. And, as a matter of "routine," Chessman was sentenced to the gas chamber.

At the time, no one in the courtroom—not even Chessman—could imagine how far from routine this case was. Caryl Chessman would spend the next 12 years of his life on death row—longer than any other person. He would become famous throughout the world. And his name would become a lasting symbol of one man's determination to fight an injustice.

Caryl Chessman had been in trouble with the law since he was a teenager. By the time he was 18, he had been sent to reform school four times for stealing. When he was older, he was arrested and convicted of armed robbery and spent time in San Quentin prison.

In January 1948, Chessman was arrested in Los Angeles and charged with several counts of assault, kidnapping, and rape. The police accused Chessman of being the notorious Red Light Bandit—a criminal they'd been pursuing for some time.

The Red Light Bandit was a man who had been terrorizing couples who parked in lovers' lanes. He had a flashing light on his car like the ones used on police cars. Pretending to be a police officer, the man would pull alongside a couples' car. Then he'd rob and sometimes assault them. In two particular cases, the Bandit kidnapped and brutally raped two women.

Chessman denied all the charges against him. At his trial, he asked the judge to allow him to defend himself. Chessman was an intelligent man— his IQ was 136—and he didn't want to hire a lawyer. The judge granted his request.

Based on the testimony of the victims, Chessman was convicted. And he was sentenced under the rules of California's "Little Lindbergh Law."

This law was passed after Charles Lindbergh's son was kidnapped and killed in the 1930s. It provided the death sentence for anyone found guilty of a kidnaping that involved bodily harm. So, although Chessman was not convicted of killing anyone, he was still sentenced to death.

> # By the late 1950s, Chessman had spent nearly ten years on death row.

From the moment he was sentenced, Chessman began his battle to overturn his conviction. He hired lawyers, and together they began the appeals process. One appeal was based on irregularities at his trial. Another protested the harshness of his sentence. It claimed that the death penalty was cruel and unusual punishment and thus forbidden by the constitution. Chessman won his first execution reprieve in March 1952.

A Best-Selling Author

But Chessman did more than file legal appeals. He had lots of time on death row. So he began to write. Over the next several years he wrote three books. One of them, *Cell 2455 Death Row* became a best seller that was translated into many languages. It turned his case into an international cause.

By the late 1950s Chessman had spent nearly ten years on death row. He had won reprieve after reprieve from execution. And he had become an expert on criminal law.

Now, many people at home and abroad began to take up Chessman's cause. Some said Chessman was innocent. They believed he had been convicted on weak testimony. Others were just flatly against capital punishment. They claimed that the death penalty was cruel and unusual punishment.

Chessman continued to fight his conviction. His case went back and forth through state and federal courts, longer than any other case in legal history. But, by the end of the decade all legal avenues seemed to have closed.

Chessman's last hope was the governor of California, Edmund G. Brown. Now only he could save Chessman by granting him a reprieve. The California Supreme Court could have recommended clemency and permanently saved Chessman. But the court had already voted twice before not to intervene.

In February 1960, Governor Brown granted Chessman a 60-day reprieve. The governor had been receiving up to 1,000 messages a day urging him to do so. Brown then asked the California legislature to consider abolishing the death penalty for good. But the legislature refused.

Chessman's lawyers tried one more time to save him. They filed another appeal with the California Supreme Court. But once again the court denied the motion.

On May 2, 1960, Caryl Chessman calmly left his prison cell and walked into the gas chamber at San Quentin. Outside the prison, and in cities around the world, people gathered to protest his execution. But this time it was to no avail.

Caryl Chessman died shortly after 10:00 A.M. He maintained his innocence to the very end. Before his death he had held a press conference in prison. He told the press that he had an overwhelming desire to "demonstrate that gas chambers and executions have no place in our civilized society."

Chessman fought his battle for 12 years. He won nine stays of execution, more than any other condemned man. In the end, however, he lost his fight. But for many death penalty opponents, his courage and determination will always be remembered. ∎

People throughout the world pleaded for clemency for Caryl Chessman in 1960.

The Kennedy Years: A Thousand Days that Stirred a Nation

From the very first moments of his presidency, John F. Kennedy seemed to inspire the nation. In his inaugural speech he had said, "The torch has been passed to a new generation. Let us begin anew. Ask not what your country can do for you. Ask what you can do for your country."

John Kennedy brought to the presidency a style of leadership Americans had never witnessed before. At 43, he was the youngest person ever to be elected president, and he was the first Catholic ever to reach that office. He was witty and charming. He was as handsome as his wife, Jacqueline, was beautiful.

The American people quickly grew to love this vigorous, charming man. He revived their hopes for a better world. Right from the start, Kennedy promised to change things. He promised to "get the country moving again."

In the 1950s many people had lived in fear. They were afraid of communists. They were afraid of nuclear war. Others became bored with government—they no longer cared who was in office. Kennedy wanted to change all that.

The new president didn't waste any time getting to work. On his first day in office he issued an executive order. This order doubled the amount of food the government gave to poor people. And that was just the beginning. As his term continued, he created many more pro-grams for the poor and unemployed. And he worked to get equal rights for minorities.

Kennedy helped America get ahead in the space race. It was his idea to ask Congress for the money to put a man on the moon. And he was one of the few presidents to actively support the arts. He set up the Advisory Council on the Arts.

He also started the Food for Peace program and the Peace Corps. He launched these programs to help poor people in other countries. It was his belief that these programs would help new nations gain strength and independence.

Kennedy was very different from the man he succeeded in office, Dwight Eisenhower. Eisen-

At his inauguration President Kennedy promised to lead the nation into a "New Frontier."

hower once said that it didn't matter who was president. He said that government policy should not depend on any individual. But Kennedy believed the opposite. He thought that each president should govern in his own way, that each president should be different.

The advisers Kennedy chose were also different. Most of Eisenhower's advisers were from the business world. But Kennedy selected only a few from business. Many of his advisers were university professors.

Kennedy changed the nation's whole defense strategy. Eisenhower insisted that America should have the best nuclear weapons. He thought they would protect America from its enemies. If attacked, the United States could then respond by launching its missiles. So Eisenhower increased the number of nuclear missiles. But there was only a limited

President Kennedy laughs at a reporter's question during his news conference in January 1963. The handsome young president was known for his witty humor.

"The torch has been passed to a new generation," Kennedy said.

amount of defense money to spend. So he had to reduce the number of U.S. combat troops.

Kennedy, on the other hand, didn't want nuclear weapons to be America's first line of defense. He wanted to have another choice. He thought there was still a need for rifle-carrying soldiers. So he spent less money on nuclear weapons, and he increased the number of troops.

Popular With the Press

The press was pleasantly surprised by Kennedy. They were used to Eisenhower. The former army general always avoided reporters. He didn't want to publicize many of the things he did. But Kennedy welcomed them into his home. And he allowed them in his office. Reporters could often be found with him at the White House swimming pool.

Kennedy's beautiful wife Jacqueline—he called her Jackie—brought a glamorous new image to the White House. She also made many changes. For years, people had thought of White House parties as stuffy and boring. But Mrs. Kennedy started a new style of entertaining.

She invited many different kinds of people to her frequent parties. Many were politicians, of course, but other professionals such as artists, entertainers, and sports personalities were invited too.

Mrs. Kennedy also gave a televised tour of the White House. Millions of viewers were thrilled to get a look at the First Family's home. It was the first time television cameras had ever been inside the president's living quarters.

Many people thought the president and his wife were romantic figures. They were both well-educated, cultured people. They both came from wealthy families. And they had many wealthy friends. So their lives seemed even more exciting

than most presidential couples.

They also shocked some people. Other presidential couples were almost always together. The public expected the Kennedys to be that way as well. But the Kennedys frequently went on separate trips. There had never been a president and first lady like the Kennedys.

But behind the romantic image, there always was the heavy and very real responsibility of Kennedy's office.

And in October 1962, that responsibility weighed more heavily on the young president than at any other time.

There was a crisis in Cuba. The Soviet Union had put missiles on that tiny island only 90 miles from America's shores. The United States demanded they be removed. And the world held its breath. People everywhere prayed that the two strongest nations would not set in motion events that could destroy themselves—and the entire planet as well. ■

President Kennedy meets with his cabinet and advisers during the Cuban missile crisis in October 1962.

The Cuban Missile Crisis:
On the Brink of Nuclear War

Something had to be done—and quickly. Russia had to be stopped. The American government couldn't allow offensive missiles to be installed in Cuba—just 90 miles from the United States.

It was October 22, 1962. President Kennedy was sitting at a White House meeting looking at some frightening pictures. These pictures showed that the Soviets were building offensive missile bases on the tiny island nation of Cuba. Photographed by a U-2 spy plane, the pictures showed that the bases were almost finished. No one at the meeting doubted that nuclear missiles would be pointed at the United States.

President Kennedy decided to go on television. He wanted to speak directly to the American people. The Soviets had deliberately deceived America, he said. They had said the missile bases would only be used for defensive weapons. But that wasn't true, and Kennedy was angry. He warned Cuba not to launch any missiles. He said that even if they launched a defensive missile, the United States would consider it an attack. Then America would launch its own missiles against Cuba.

Actually, Kennedy had known about the bases eight days before he spoke on television. But he had kept it a secret. He wanted time to decide what to do. In fact, Kennedy knew much earlier that something was happening in Cuba. But at first it wasn't clear what the Soviets were up to. The Russians had never built any missile bases outside of their own country before. So, at first, no one in the U.S. government suspected that was what they were doing.

Then the U-2 photographs showed that defensive missile bases were being built.

So the president held a press conference. He said that if the Soviets turned Cuba into an offensive base, America would have to protect itself. Cuba and the Soviets said that wouldn't happen.

But then some Cuban refugees told the U.S. government that the sites were for offensive nuclear missiles. Russian ships were bringing the materials to Cuba, they said.

Even with this information Kennedy couldn't do anything. He had to have proof that the bases were for offensive missiles. So on October 14, more U-2 pictures were taken. This time they showed that some of the bases were definitely intended for offensive missiles.

Kennedy called in his advisers. They knew they had only about ten days before the bases would be finished. Then the missiles would be ready to strike America.

After lengthy discussions, the president decided on a naval blockade. American ships would keep the Soviets from bringing more materials into Cuba. This would keep the Russians from finishing the bases. In addition, the United States brought its photographic evidence to the United Nations to prove their charges against the Soviets.

A Very Tense Two Days

When all this news became public, many people around the world became frightened. It seemed that America and Russia might fight a nuclear war. For two days, the world waited tensely. Then it looked as if the Soviets might back down.

Soviet premier Nikita Khrushchev personally called two Americans who were in Moscow. Kennedy thought this was a good sign. Next, the Soviet ships nearest Cuba slowed down and changed course. They had

---

Khrushchev knew his gamble had failed.

---

decided not to challenge the blockade. One Soviet ship did run the blockade. But the United States knew the ship was only a tanker. It wasn't carrying any weapons. So it was allowed to pass.

By October 26, Khrushchev realized that the United States was prepared to invade Cuba if he didn't back down. He knew his gamble had

failed. That day Soviet officials talked to an American reporter. They said the Soviets would remove their missiles from Cuba. They also promised that Russia would never again give Cuba offensive weapons. But the Russians wanted something in exchange. The United States must promise not to invade Cuba.

The reporter delivered the Soviet message to Kennedy. Then the Soviets sent another, different message to the president. It was less friendly. It seemed like Khrushchev had changed his mind.

Kennedy was confused. Then one of his aides figured out what happened. The second message was actually sent first! But it had taken longer to reach Washington.

So the president decided to ignore the second message. He sent a note to Khrushchev. He said America would agree to the first idea.

On October 28 Khrushchev accepted. And the most serious crisis of the cold war had come to a peaceful end. ∎

This aerial photo, taken in October 1962, shows the Soviet missile base erected at San Cristobal, Cuba.

Martin Luther King, Jr., addresses a huge crowd in Washington, D.C., during the march for civil rights on August 28, 1963.

200,000 People With a Dream March on Washington

They had come from every corner of the land—more than 200,000 men, women, and children, whites and Negroes, rich and poor. They were in Washington, D.C., for one reason. They had come to announce that it was time for all Americans to be treated equally, regardless of their color. It was time for all Americans to be granted their civil rights.

The march on Washington took place on August 28, 1963. It was the climax of years of nonviolent struggle to achieve civil rights. The main inspiration of this movement was Dr. Martin Luther King, Jr., a Baptist minister. Ever since the mid-1950s, King had dedicated his life to bringing about racial justice in America.

Dr. King had first come to national attention back in December 1955. He had helped organize a local car pool to transport Negroes who were boycotting a bus company in Montgomery, Alabama. The Negro community was boycotting the buses to protest the arrest of a Negro woman named Rosa Parks. Parks had been arrested for refusing to give up her bus seat to a white man. Her refusal was against local law.

Segregation Called "Unconstitutional"

During the year-long boycott, Dr. King and other organizers were jailed in Montgomery. They had been charged with operating an illegal transport service. But the boycott was successful.

Meanwhile, Rosa Parks had taken her case to the United States Supreme Court and had won. The Court said that the Alabama law requiring segregation on buses was unconstitutional. This was a major victory in the struggle for civil rights. But it was just the beginning.

In 1957, King and other Negro clergymen formed the Southern Christian Leadership Conference (SCLC). This group was intended to coordinate the work of many civil rights groups. King urged Negroes to use only peaceful means to achieve their goals. He preached nonviolent resistance. He knew that passive resistance, as practiced by Mahatma Gandhi, had won independence for India.

In 1960 a group of Negro and white college students organized the Student Nonviolent Coordinating Committee (SNCC). They planned to help in the civil rights movement by staging sit-ins, boycotts, marches, and "freedom rides." They were joined by young people from the SCLC, CORE (Congress of Racial Equality) and the NAACP (National Association for the Advancement of Colored People.)

The freedom rides were organized in order to test the desegregation laws on interstate buses. The freedom riders rode buses all over the South. Many of the riders were beaten up. And buses were often wrecked. But the freedom rides helped to make sure that the new laws were being enforced.

In October 1960, King was arrested with 33 young people. They had been protesting segregation at the lunch counter of an Atlanta, Georgia, department store. Charges were dropped. But King was sentenced to prison anyway. He was charged with a minor traffic offense and violating his probation.

By this time, King had become a nationally known figure. He had attracted a growing number of enthusiastic supporters—Negroes and white liberals—all across the nation. And his supporters now feared for King's safety. So they worked to get King released from prison. And thanks to the efforts of Democratic presidential candidate John F. Kennedy, he was.

When Kennedy became president in January 1961, he took some steps toward granting Negroes equal rights. He appointed Negroes to several important federal government jobs. He issued an executive order ending segregation in public housing projects built with federal money. And he set up an Equal Employment Opportunity committee. But despite these steps, by 1963, life for many American Negroes had not greatly improved.

In April 1963, King led a campaign to end segregation at lunch counters and in hiring practices in Birmingham, Alabama. The protests lasted for weeks. The city police, led by Eugene "Bull" Connor, used police dogs, fire hoses, and electric cattle prods to finally break up the demonstrations. King and hundreds of his supporters were jailed. The violence was reported on TV news and in the newspapers. Many Americans were outraged at the brutal treatment of the demonstrators.

After the April demonstrations more violence occurred in Birmingham. Four Negro girls were killed when the church they were

attending was bombed. That same day, two Negro youths were shot to death in a different part of town. The violence was terrible. But it had the unintended effect of winning more white support for the civil rights movement.

In June 1963, President Kennedy sent a civil rights bill to Congress. There, a bitter fight broke out between supporters and opponents

It was time for all Americans to be granted their civil rights.

of the bill. King and the other civil rights leaders then decided to organize a march on Washington. Their purpose was to protest discrimination and to urge Congress to pass the civil rights bill.

So on August 28, 1963, more than 200,000 people arrived in the nation's capital. Many came on "freedom buses" and "freedom trains" from cities all across the country.

At the Lincoln Memorial, they heard several addresses, including

one by Martin Luther King, Jr. In one of the most moving and memorable speeches in American history, King declared:

"I have a dream that one day this nation will rise up and live out the true meaning of its creed . . . that all men are created equal. I have a dream that my four little children will one day live in a nation where they will not be judged by the color of their skin, but by the content of their character. I have a dream today. And if America is to be a great nation, this must become true. So let freedom ring. From the prodigious hilltops of New Hampshire, let freedom ring. From the heightening Alleghenies of Pennsylvania, let freedom ring. But not only that; let freedom ring from Stone Mountain of Georgia. Let freedom ring from every hill and molehill of Mississippi. And when this happens, when we let it ring, we will speed that day when all of God's children, black men and white men, Jews and Gentiles, Protestants and Catholics, will be able to join hands and sing in the words of the old Negro spiritual: 'Free at last, free at last, Thank God Almighty, we're free at last.'" ■

Thousands upon thousands of civil rights marchers parade down Constitution Avenue during the march on Washington, D.C.

Kennedy Assassinated

Nation Stunned By News From Dallas

The nation was stunned. One minute their popular young president was smiling and waving to cheering crowds from his presidential motorcade. The next minute John F. Kennedy was dead.

It was a clear day in Dallas on November 22, 1963. President Kennedy and his wife were riding in an open car. Texas governor John Connally and his wife were with them. Connally was also wounded in the attack on Kennedy. He watched in horror as the president was killed.

"We had just turned the corner," Connally said later. "We heard a shot. I turned to my left to look in the back seat. The president had slumped. He had said nothing. Then there was another shot—the president was hit again. And Mrs. Kennedy said, 'Oh my God! They killed my husband.'"

Kennedy slumped into his wife's arms. She cradled him there as a Secret Service man jumped onto the car. Then they sped off in the blood-spattered limousine.

The president was taken to Parkland Hospital in Dallas. The doctors there worked feverishly to revive him. But it was hopeless. He had been shot twice. One bullet passed through his neck, and the other crushed his skull.

Vice-President Lyndon B. Johnson was riding in another car. When Kennedy was shot, the vice president was immediately surrounded by Secret Service men. It was their job to protect him from another sniper's bullet. Later that day, Lyndon Johnson was sworn in as president. The ceremony was performed on Air Force One before it flew the presidential party back to Washington.

Dallas police immediately began the most intensive murder investigation of the century. Only hours after the shooting, they arrested Lee Harvey Oswald. He insisted that he had killed no one. But investigators believed otherwise.

The shots had come from the sixth floor of the Texas School Book Depository building. And police found a high-powered rifle there. Its bullets matched the ones fired at the president. The gun belonged to Oswald. And Oswald worked in the book depository.

Oswald had been in the Marine Corps. He was known to be a good marksman. Circumstances indicated that he committed the crime. But there were still doubts. There was only one eyewitness. He said he saw a gun in the window of the book depository. But no one clearly saw the man behind the gun.

Mrs. Kennedy said, "Oh, my God, they killed my husband."

There was endless speculation. Might there have been a second gunman? Could Oswald be in the pay of the Soviet Union? Was he hired by someone else? Or did he act entirely on his own? But the most important question of all was: Why would anyone want the president dead?

President Johnson appointed a federal commission to investigate the crime. The Warren Commission spent months pouring over testimony. In the end, though, they seemed to have learned nothing new. Their conclusion was that Lee Harvey Oswald, acting alone, killed the president.

Many people were not satisfied with the findings of the Warren Commission. A lot of people said that Oswald could not possibly have acted alone. Or, even if he had, another person (or persons) probably hired him to kill Kennedy.

But despite all the doubts, no clear-cut evidence was ever established to disprove the conclusions of the Commission. Yet, years later, the events surrounding the murder of John F. Kennedy continue to be a subject of controversy—mixed with tragedy. ∎

Seconds after shots hit President Kennedy, a Secret Service man jumped onto the president's limousine.

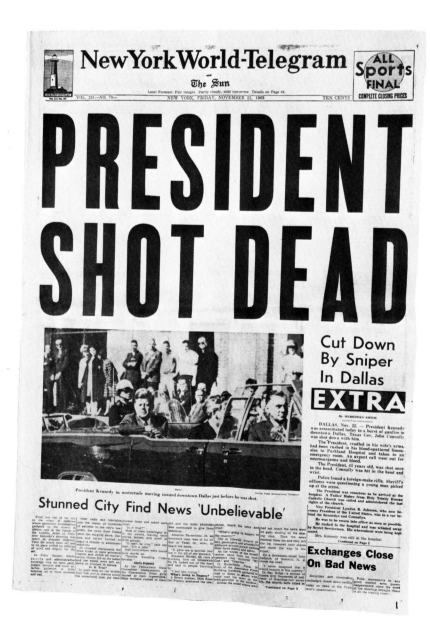

The front page of the *New York World-Telegram* relates the tragic news of November 22, 1963.

Prelude to Murder

Like all presidents, President Kennedy routinely received threats on his life. But few of them were ever taken seriously. Such threats were accepted as a part of public life.

But some of his aides were worried about the Texas trip scheduled for November 1963. They didn't want him to go to Dallas. Besides the death threats that had been made, there were other warning signs in the air. Four weeks earlier, UN Ambassador Adlai Stevenson was in Dallas. He had been roughed up by demonstrators there.

But Kennedy said he wasn't afraid of physical danger. He was already going to Houston, San Antonio, and Fort Worth. He felt he couldn't go to those cities and not go to Dallas. So the Dallas visit was scheduled.

The day Kennedy arrived in Texas there was another warning. The Dallas *Morning News* printed an anti-Kennedy ad. But the crowds cheered the president in San Antonio. And he got a warm welcome in Fort Worth.

Before leaving for Dallas, the president stopped briefly at his hotel room. There he and his wife talked to an aide about his safety. Kennedy said that he knew he could easily be killed. But he said he had to take that chance. He felt that a president had to be courageous.

That afternoon the president made the short trip to Dallas. As his motorcade entered the city, the crowds grew larger. They waved and cheered. Kennedy was happy. The presidential limousine turned off Main Street and onto Elm Street. It was headed toward the Texas School Book Depository—and a sniper with a rifle in a sixth floor window.

An Assassin's Death

It was a nightmare of confusion and disbelief. Only 48 hours had passed since President Kennedy's assassination. And now his suspected killer was dead too. The assassin himself had been assassinated.

Lee Harvey Oswald had been captured only a few hours after Kennedy was shot on Friday afternoon. The police took him to a jail in Dallas. But there were threats made against Oswald's life. So the police decided to move him to another jail.

On Sunday morning the police escorted Oswald to a waiting armored car. The passageway was packed with a crowd of journalists. Television cameras were recording the scene when suddenly a man stepped in front of Oswald. Before anyone could stop him, he pulled out a pistol and fired a shot.

The bullet hit Oswald in the stomach. Millions of television viewers watched as he clutched himself in agony.

Oswald was rushed to Parkland Hospital—the same place that President Kennedy had been taken. He was treated in an emergency room, just a few steps away from where Kennedy had died. There Oswald also died.

Oswald's killer was a local nightclub owner named Jack Ruby. He had hidden the gun in his clothing. Then he had fired it at point-blank range when Oswald got close to him.

Now that Oswald could never be brought to trial, many questions would have to go unanswered. But there were a few things that were known about him. Lee Harvey Oswald was a known Communist. He had been a U.S. marine and a good marksman. But the Marine Corps had court-martialed him twice and finally discharged him.

Then Oswald spent several months in Russia where he learned the Russian language. He'd even applied for Soviet citizenship. He'd worked in a Russian factory and married a Russian woman. Records showed that before the assassination, Oswald had bought the gun that was used to kill the president. Then he had gone to Mexico City.

Some people believed that he went to the Soviet embassy in Mexico. They think he might have talked to the Soviets about an assassination plan. But no one knows what he really did there. It is known, however, that the papers announced Kennedy's trip to Dallas while Oswald was in Mexico. When Oswald came back to the United States, he got a job at the Texas School Book Depository in Dallas. Oswald was in the depository when the shots were fired from the building. The case against him was a strong one. But no one can be sure of his guilt.

Jack Ruby was convicted of killing Oswald. But he was a very ill man. He died while his case was being appealed.

When Oswald died, America's hope of knowing the whole truth died, too. The full details of President Kennedy's assassination would remain a mystery forever. ■

Accused presidential assassin Lee Harvey Oswald (center) is shown moments before he was shot and killed by Jack Ruby.

An honor guard drapes an American flag over the casket of the slain president. The riderless horse that symbolizes a lost leader waits for the journey to begin.

The Nation Mourns a Fallen Leader

President Kennedy's death shocked the world. By the thousands, grieving people came to Washington to mourn him. Many of the mourners were heads of state from all over the world. Many more were ordinary Americans.

Kennedy's body had been returned immediately to the nation's capital. There, in the East Room of the White House, he lay in state. An honor guard stood by his coffin day and night. The weather outside was dreary and wet.

Then on November 24, he was taken to the Capitol rotunda. Thousands lined Pennsylvania Avenue. They watched the procession take the fallen president down the street to the Capitol building. His coffin was draped with an American flag. It was drawn by six gray horses. They were followed by a riderless horse—boots turned backward in the stirrups. This was a symbol that the horse's rider was dead.

Inside the Capitol, hundreds of thousands came to pay their last respects to their dead president. Many people cried as they filed past his coffin.

On November 25, the president's funeral was held at St. Matthew's Cathedral. Officials from more than 90 countries came to pay their last respects. Then he took one last trip to Arlington National Cemetery across the Potomac River from Washington, D.C. There he was buried with full military honors.

Jacqueline Kennedy, the president's widow, lit the eternal flame that still burns over his grave.

The Kennedy family received hundreds of thousands of letters and telegrams of sympathy from all over the world. For days after the funeral, thousands of people came to visit Kennedy's grave. On Thanksgiving Day alone, more than 200,000 people came to pay their respects.

Today, thousands of people still come to visit his grave every year. They file past the eternal flame and remember the handsome young president who died too soon. ∎

August 1965. Almost a full city block appears to be bombed out after four days of burning, looting, and rioting in the Negro district of Watts in Los Angeles.

America's Cities Burn

The Long, Hot Summers of Rage

The summers of the midsixties saw ghettos torched and a new awareness burned into America's consciousness. And it was all on television. Americans watched scene after scene of angry, young Negroes clashing over and over again with police and national guardsmen. Huge sections of America's cities were in ruins. Some rioters were killed and thousands arrested. Policemen were weary and injured. Whole streets were on fire.

Up through the early 1960s, some progress had been made in civil rights for Negroes. Now legislation had desegregated some schools. Poll taxes and literacy tests had been eliminated. President Johnson signed a national civil rights law that further outlawed racial discrimination. Dr. Martin Luther King, Jr., and other Negro leaders were demonstrating for changes.

Still there were many whites who did not want equality for Negroes. And many Negroes weren't willing to wait for slow change. Or changes that might not even come. They felt they had been patient long enough. Too many Negroes still lived in poor and neglected parts of America's cities. The unemployment rate in these ghettos was about three times higher than the rate for whites. Tensions and frustrations were as high as the crime rates. It seemed that urban warfare was about to erupt at any time.

> "Our nation is moving toward two societies—one black, one white."

When it finally did, people had to ask themselves some hard questions. How did America's cities become so divided and torn? What could make people strike out so violently against their own communities? How did America reach the point where its citizens could watch their cities burn on the evening news?

One hundred years after the Civil War, millions of Negroes were living in northern cities. Most lived in large ghettos or isolated neighborhoods. These people were generally poor and often hungry. The ghettos had many problems such as poor transportation, little crime control, undependable garbage collection, and lack of money to operate good schools.

The Negroes' living conditions were miserable compared to other residents of the same city or nearby suburbs. Civil rights laws had not improved these conditions. President Johnson's "War on Poverty" had come too late with too little. The money from all the poverty programs combined amounted only to about $25.00 per person.

Instead of Dr. King's nonviolent type of protest, some Negroes wanted to get action with violence. They wanted to confront the government. They wanted to have political power right away. New slogans began to appear like "black is beautiful." Negroes started to call themselves "blacks." They were proud of their color and of their African heritage.

Riots started in the summer of 1964 in a New York ghetto neighborhood called Harlem. Soon they spread to other ghettos in New York City and then to other cities.

A Neighborhood in Ruins

By the summer of 1965, the riots had spread to the West Coast. One neighborhood in Los Angeles had been simmering all summer. Watts seemed ready to boil over. And suddenly, it did.

It hadn't taken much to start it off. A policeman arrested a young Negro man for reckless driving. An angry crowd gathered around the officer. The arrested man's mother arrived at the scene. She began shouting at the policeman.

The officer realized that he was in trouble. So he tried to radio for help. At that point the riot started.

For six days in August, Negro rioters destroyed houses and businesses in their own neighborhoods. They looted appliance stores and supermarkets. They broke windows, set fires, and attacked bystanders.

Firemen tried to put out the blazing buildings. But there were too many fires and too few firefighters. And there was a further danger. Snipers fired shots at them from the tops of buildings.

Then the riots spread. At first the rioting remained in an eight-block area. Then it grew to 150 blocks. More than 10,000 national guardsmen were brought in to restore order. They sealed off the area so that the riots couldn't spread any farther. By the time it was over, the numbers were staggering. In all, more than 30 people were killed. Hundreds were injured. And nearly 4,000 were arrested.

The Watts riot was America's worst case of racial violence. And it proved to be just the first of many riots to come in that summer of 1965. A similar riot started in Chicago about the same time.

The nation watched in disbelief. People could see their cities burning on television. Where would the violence end? And when?

Then it ended as suddenly as it began. There were no more riots that summer. And the following summer was fairly quiet. But in the summer of 1967, far bigger and more violent race riots erupted. Like the Watts riots, the violence came suddenly in the long, hot summer.

The summer's violence began in Boston. The pattern was the same as the Watts riot of 1965. This time police were called to control a group of women. The women had gathered to peacefully protest welfare policies. When asked to leave, they refused. The confrontation became angry. Other people gathered around. The police tried to use force. The people reacted with force. The incident exploded into a full riot.

Again, Negroes looted and burned the ghetto where they lived. Then rioting broke out in other American cities. All that summer, violence ripped through the big cities.

The race riots of these two summers all followed similar patterns. They occurred on a hot summer day when: Negroes were already upset or frustrated about something, the police were called, a crowd gathered, the police tried to control the situation, and the crowd became violent.

In just that way a small incident grew into uncontrolled looting and rioting.

In 1967, more than 164 cities in 32 states were torn by riots. When it was over, 83 people were dead, 3,400 had been injured, and 18,800 had been arrested.

No part of the country was spared. Birmingham was hit in the South. New York was burned in the North. And San Francisco was looted in the West.

Newark, New Jersey, was one of the cities hit hardest. And in Detroit, rioters destroyed 18 city blocks.

President Johnson appointed a special commission to study the riots. They tried to find out the causes of all the violence. The commission reported that, "Our nation is moving toward two societies, one black, one white." The commission concluded that the government should work to rebuild the ghettos. America should treat blacks and whites as equals so that future riots will not occur. ∎

A Michigan National Guardsman's bayonet stands out against a background of destruction. The scene is the west side of Detroit after four nights of rioting by blacks.

Hawks Versus Doves— A Divided Nation

Not since the Civil War had America faced such a challenge. As the nation became more involved in the war in Vietnam, peace at home was threatened. America seemed to be splitting in half. A nation of "doves" were on one side, and "hawks" were on the other.

The doves were opposed to American involvement in the war. They felt that the U.S. governmental policies were immoral. They said the United States should not be supporting a "corrupt and undemocratic" government in South Vietnam. They maintained that the war was basically a civil war. The Vietnamese, they said, should be left to fight it out among themselves.

The hawks felt that it was unpatriotic to question government decisions. The government said it was fighting communism in Vietnam—that was reason enough to support the war. According to the hawks, people who protested the war were disloyal to their country.

The antiwar movement got started shortly after the first U.S. military actions. On August 4, 1964, President Lyndon Johnson had ordered air strikes against North Vietnam. He claimed that the North Vietnamese had attacked the U.S. Navy destroyers *Maddox* and *C. Turner Joy* in the Gulf of Tonkin. About two months later, on September 30, a big demonstration was

staged. Thousands of people gathered at the University of California in Berkeley to protest American military involvement.

On March 8, 1965, the first U.S. combat troops, about 3,500 marines, arrived in South Vietnam. Thousands more would follow. By 1969 there would be more than 543,000 U.S. troops in Vietnam.

Meanwhile, the antiwar movement began to pick up steam. At first the demonstrations were small. Opinion polls showed that at least 25 percent of the American public hadn't even heard of Vietnam. A majority of those who had, supported the president.

But as the war dragged on, each

In November 1965, a protest march in Oakland, California, drew thousands of anti-Vietnam War demonstrators.

Military police block the entrance to the Pentagon as anti-Vietnam War demonstrators taunt them. The march on the Pentagon, in October 1967, drew about 50,000 protesters.

protest march seemed to grow larger. College campuses became centers of protest activity. Students and professors held "teach-ins." At these gatherings they talked about the war. And they helped to organize the antiwar effort. Thousands of young men believed that they could not, in good conscience, participate in the war. They worried about being drafted. They knew they would have to refuse to fight in Vietnam. On October 15, 1965, a young man named David Miller became the first protester to burn his draft card.

During 1966, as more and more American soldiers were dying in Vietnamese jungles, antiwar protests greatly increased. On May 15, 1966, more than 10,000 people picketed the White House in Washington, D.C.

But the Johnson administration seemed to ignore the protests. They continued to send more soldiers to Vietnam.

Many doves were becoming outraged at the government's refusal to change its policies. When Defense Secretary Robert McNamara was asked to speak at Harvard University, in November 1966, he was unable to give his speech. He was shouted down by angry demonstrators.

Hawks were also getting angry— at the doves. For the most part, demonstrations against the war had been peaceful protests up to now. But by late 1966, many prowar demonstrators began appearing at antiwar protests. Then, what began as nasty name-calling, developed into violent confrontations between the

two groups . Such incidents would usually end with the police firing tear gas and arresting the protesters.

By early 1967 public opinion was slowly turning against the administration's war policies. In February, a survey showed that more than half the American people disapproved of the way Johnson was handling the war. But more than half of them also believed in continuing the fight against North Vietnam.

The March on the Pentagon

In March 1967, 5,000 people demonstrated in Chicago. They were led by Dr. Martin Luther King, Jr.

In April 1967, 200 draft resisters burned their draft cards in New York's Central Park. And on May 13, ⇨

1967, more than 70,000 antiwar marchers paraded down New York's Fifth Avenue.

One of the largest antiwar protests in Washington took place in October 1967. More than 50,000 people marched on the Pentagon. Among the demonstrators were members of 150 different antiwar and civil rights groups. The march began peacefully at the Lincoln Memorial on October 21. When the marchers reached the Pentagon, they found many paratroopers and policemen guarding the building. So the protesters couldn't get in.

Many people simply sat down in front of the police. They refused to move. Then tear gas was fired into the crowd. After a while, most of the protesters left. Those that remained were arrested by the police.

At the end of the year, protesters organized a "Stop the Draft Week." About 40 antiwar groups participated. Groups of demonstrators, chanting antiwar slogans, blocked induction centers around the country.

A Very Unpopular War

College students also protested the use of deadly chemicals in the war. One demonstration took place at San Jose State University in California. These students were protesting against the Dow Chemical Company. The company made napalm and other chemicals of war. Napalm was used in the war as a defoliant to strip the trees and plants of leaves. But defoliants also burned human flesh. Many Vietnamese men, women, and children were maimed or killed by napalm.

The war was becoming more and more unpopular. By March 1969 only 30 percent of the American people were still in favor of the war. The other 70 percent wanted the United States to end its involvement in Southeast Asia.

On October 15, 1969, some 250,000 marchers paraded down Pennsylvania Avenue in Washington, D.C. This was the largest antiwar demonstration of the decade. A new president, Richard M. Nixon, was sitting in the White House. His administration was no friendlier to the antiwar movement than Johnson's had been. But the marchers still hoped that their message was beginning to get through.

By the end of 1969, the first U.S. troop reductions had been announced. And Nixon had promised to further "Vietnamize" the war by bringing home U.S. troops and turning over the fighting to South Vietnamese forces. Many people in the antiwar movement had their doubts about Nixon's promises. But a bitterly divided nation could only hope for the best. ∎

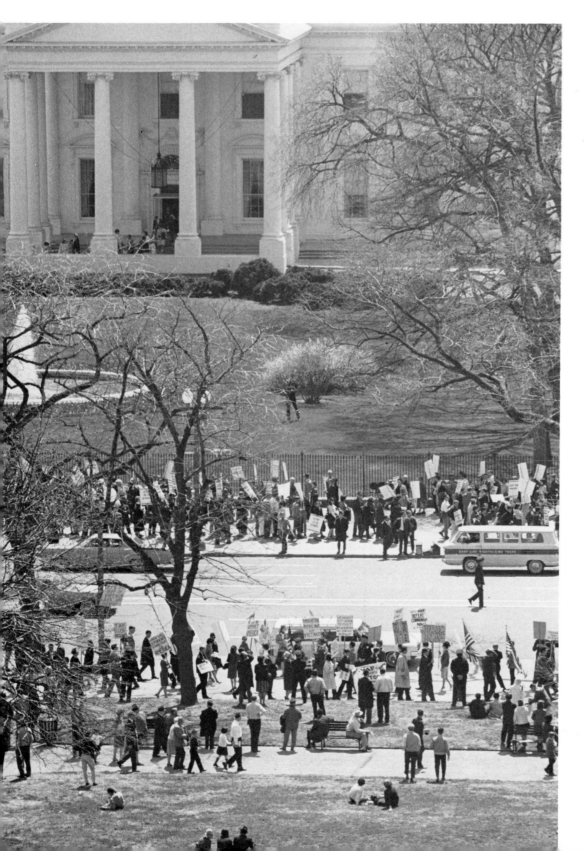

Antiwar protesters frequently demonstrated outside the White House during the sixties.

LBJ's Legislative Legacy

Was Lyndon Johnson a good president? Americans answered both yes and no. His Vietnam War policies had come under intense fire. But his domestic programs were extremely popular. Johnson had promised to build a "Great Society." In it, he said, there would be liberty for all. He was a great champion of civil rights. And he helped the poor.

In 1963 President Kennedy sent an equal rights bill to Congress. But he died before it passed. After his death, Johnson picked up the torch. He made sure the Civil Rights Act was passed and he signed it into law. The new legislation outlawed segregation. And it said the government could cut off federal funds to programs that discriminated against Negroes.

Later, Johnson sent another civil rights bill to Congress. It was the Voting Rights Act. This bill outlawed a practice that helped keep Negroes from voting. In many Southern states, Negroes had been forced to take a literacy test. They couldn't register to vote unless they passed the test. Since many Negroes failed the test, they couldn't vote. The Voting Rights Act banned such tests.

Johnson also "declared war on poverty." One of the programs he started was the "model cities" project. The model cities were to be examples of the "great society." They were to show that no situation was too hopeless to be improved. Decent housing for the poor, for example, could be built from the ruins of old, broken-down neighborhoods. Johnson quadrupled spending for urban renewal.

He also increased aid to students and schools. "Project Head Start," for example was a special program for preschool children from poor families. It was designed to help them learn the skills they would need to succeed in school. Johnson started many other education programs, as well.

But many people blamed the president for the Vietnam War. He became very unpopular. So in a televised address, on March 31, 1968, he announced he would not seek reelection.

The Johnson era was short. And it was very violent. But government spending jumped, taxes were cut, and unemployment dropped to a very low level. In spite of the social unrest, the nation had prospered. ■

President Johnson shakes hands with Dr. Martin Luther King, Jr., after signing the Civil Rights Act.

1968: Snipers, Bullets, and Bloody Riots

A terrible time of violence began in the middle 1960s. Blacks rioted in the ghettos. Anti-Vietnam War protesters demonstrated in the streets. With each new year, things got worse. The year 1968 proved to be the most violent and tragic of the decade.

In that one year, Dr. Martin Luther King, Jr., and Senator Robert Kennedy were killed by assassins. Young people demonstrated against the war. Blacks demonstrated against segregation. All that year, from spring through the election year conventions, America seemed out of control.

Martin Luther King, Jr., had dedicated his life to gaining civil rights for blacks. In the struggle for equality, he was always an advocate of nonviolent protest, a man of peace. In 1964 he had received the Nobel Peace Prize for his nonviolent approach to gaining social justice.

In 1968 Dr. King went to Memphis, Tennessee. Speaking to striking sanitation workers, he urged them not to use violence. During his career, many people had threatened

---

The year 1968 proved to be the most violent and tragic of the decade.

Dr. King's life. He had already been stabbed and stoned in New York and Chicago.

Then on April 4, a sniper shot and killed the civil rights leader. King had been talking to companions on the balcony of his Memphis hotel room. The shots had apparently come from a nearby building. The police found no one there.

After a long manhunt, police arrested James Earl Ray, an escaped convict. He was convicted and sentenced to 99 years in prison.

The nation was shocked by the assassination. Many people feared a violent reaction from blacks to the murder. Dr. King had been a moderating influence to racial tension—and now he was gone. As feared, King's death triggered a storm of racial violence all across America. There were ghetto riots and looting in more than 100 cities.

Others peacefully mourned King's killing. President Johnson designated a national day of mourning. All over the country, memorial services were held for King. More than 50,000 people gathered in Atlanta for King's funeral. Among those who visited his graveside was New York senator Robert F. Kennedy.

Kennedy was running for president that year. On June 5 he had just won the California primary election. It was an important victory. He went to the Ambassador Hotel in Los Angeles to give his victory speech. After the speech, he walked through the crowd toward an exit. He was smiling and shaking hands as he went.

Then a man holding a gun pushed through the crowd. He aimed and fired. Kennedy fell. Then more shots were fired, and five other people fell—wounded.

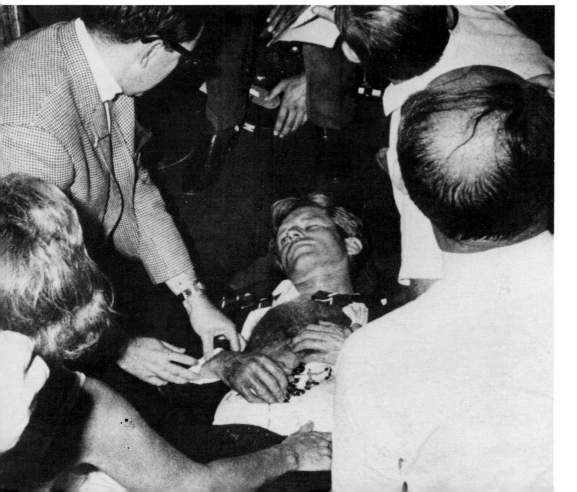

Senator Robert F. Kennedy lies mortally wounded on the floor of the Ambassador Hotel after he was gunned down in June 1968.

Chicago police and antiwar demonstrators clashed violently outside the Democratic National Convention in August 1968.

Hotel workers grabbed the gunman. They pinned him down and held him until police arrived.

Emotions flared. Some people wanted to kill the assassin on the spot. Others wanted to turn him over to police.

Kennedy was rushed to the hospital. One bullet had struck him behind the right ear. Another went under his arm. A third hit him in the neck. Doctors operated on him for nearly four hours. But his wounds were too severe. He died within hours.

The gunman was a Palestinian from Jordan named Sirhan Bishara Sirhan. It never became clear why he killed Kennedy. But the senator's death was yet another tragedy for America. Kennedy had been the front-runner for the Democratic presidential nomination in 1968. Now he was gone.

Chaos in Chicago

In March, President Lyndon Johnson had decided not to run for a second term. The Vietnam War and disturbances at home had worn him out. In addition, his popularity was very low. Vice-President Hubert Humphrey had decided to run for the Democrats. He had the backing of the president. Humphrey supported Johnson's policy of continuing the Vietnam War.

The Democrats held their nominating convention in Chicago that August. The party was divided into two factions. The "hawks," those who wanted to continue the war, were in the majority. In 1968, the United States had nearly 500,000 troops in Vietnam. Nearly 30,000 men had been killed. U.S. and South Vietnamese troops were losing important battles.

Senator Eugene McCarthy of Minnesota was also running for president. He claimed that the war was not moral. People dissatisfied with Johnson and the war supported McCarthy. He represented the "peace now" or "dove" faction of the Democratic party. This group wanted to stop bombing Vietnam and nearby countries. They demanded immediate withdrawal of American troops.

A Police Riot

Outside the convention, many groups had come to protest the war. They marched in the streets to make the Democrats pay attention to their views.

Chicago police and National Guard troops were sent to control the demonstrators. But the police became impatient with the noisy, disorderly crowd.

So they charged the demonstrators, and threw tear gas at them. And they beat many protesters with billy clubs. Americans saw much of the protest on television. Seeing the violence the police used against the marchers made many viewers sympathetic with the protesters. Maybe they didn't agree with "peace now." But they didn't like the use of unnecessary force, either.

The violence outside the convention worked against the Democrats. Many people saw the Democrats as unable to keep order. The violence emphasized how divided they were. In the end, the convention nominated Hubert Humphrey as their candidate. The "hawks" had won.

By comparison, the Republican convention was calm. Richard M. Nixon, who was Eisenhower's vice president during the 1950s, was supported by most delegates. Nixon claimed to represent the "silent majority." He said these Americans supported law and order. But Nixon did promise to end the war in Vietnam. He said he wanted "peace with honor." And he also wanted to crack down on crime in the United States.

Americans were deeply divided on how to end U.S. involvement in the war. However, they did want to stop violence and crime in America. People wondered if Humphrey would be a strong leader able to maintain order.

Nixon was elected president in November 1968. Student protests against the war continued. But Americans hoped that a new year would see an end to the violence and unrest that had swept across America in 1968. ∎

A chimpanzee named Ham was the first "living American" to orbit the earth in January 1961. Shown here in his tiny space capsule, Ham looks as if he enjoyed the trip.

The Early Space Race

America Ranks Second Best

It was the fall of 1960, and America had suffered another defeat in the space race. The Russians celebrated the success of their fifth Sputnik. They were the first to send a live dog into orbit—and successfully bring him back!

Russia launched its first satellite on October 4, 1957. Sputnik 1 was the first artificial satellite ever put into space. The first Soviet rockets were really missiles, designed to carry bombs. The Russians had been working on them since 1947. The first missile that could travel between continents was called the R-7. It could carry a two-ton bomb over 4,000 miles.

The Soviets wanted to demonstrate their missile to America. They wanted to prove that they had this weapon. But they didn't want to attack the United States. So they built Sputnik 1. Then they attached it to their missile and fired it into space.

America was shocked by Sputnik 1. Americans had believed that they were first in technology. They thought their country had a military advantage over Russia. But Sputnik 1 changed everything.

Now many Americans were afraid. They thought the Soviets might be preparing to drop bombs from space. They believed that America needed to catch up with Russia—and to do it quickly. Then there would be no need to worry.

At first, the United States was slow to respond. Its first entry in the space race was a three-and-one-half pound satellite. At launch, it's three-stage rocket rose only a few feet off the ground. Then it crashed and burned.

In January 1958, the United States finally launched a successful satellite, Explorer I. The satellite was very small, but at least the United States had joined the space race.

By mid-1958, the Soviets had launched three Sputniks. The United States had successfully launched only the Explorer I and another satellite, Vanguard I.

The American public began demanding a manned flight. So President Eisenhower created the National Aeronautics and Space Administration. NASA's job was to put a man in space. Now the race was on in earnest. But NASA wasn't ready to put a man in space. Thousands of tests had to be made first.

By 1961 things still didn't look good for America. NASA had tried to launch 28 satellites in the past three years. Only eight of them were successful.

Finally, in January 1961, America had an important success. A chimpanzee named "Ham" was put in a tiny space capsule and launched into orbit.

The capsule made one complete circuit around the earth. Then it came home safely. Ham became the first "living American" in space.

But Ham was still only an animal. The next step was to launch a man into space.

Alan Shepard was supposed to have been the first man in space. At least according to America's schedule. He would take that historic trip in his Mercury space capsule. Since the capsule could hold only a single man, he would take the trip alone. But then the plan changed. The

Mercury wouldn't be ready to take off in March 1961. The flight was rescheduled for May. In the meantime, though, a Russian made the journey. On April 12, 1961, Yuri Gagarin completed one full orbit before returning to earth. Once again the Soviets were a jump ahead.

Three weeks later, on May 5, America finally launched a manned space flight. Shepard rode a rocket to a height of 116½ miles, in a flight 300 miles long that lasted 15 minutes. The United States was still behind the Soviet Union, however. America wasn't able to orbit the earth with a manned flight yet. But Shepard's flight made history—and made Americans feel better about the space race.

The United States had very ambitious plans in space travel. That same year President Kennedy had outlined what he saw as America's ultimate goal in space: put a man on the moon by the end of the decade.

But the Mercury project had to be finished before that could happen. Shepard was only the first of six astronauts in the Mercury program.

Virgil "Gus" Grissom repeated Shepard's flight in July 1961. Then in February 1962, John Glenn became the first American astronaut to orbit the earth, circling the planet three times. The last Mercury flight was in May 1963. Gordon Cooper orbited the earth 22 times in 34 hours. That was the longest period of time that any American had stayed in space.

Now it was time for the next stage of space exploration to begin. America was going to the moon. But could it beat the Soviet Union? ∎

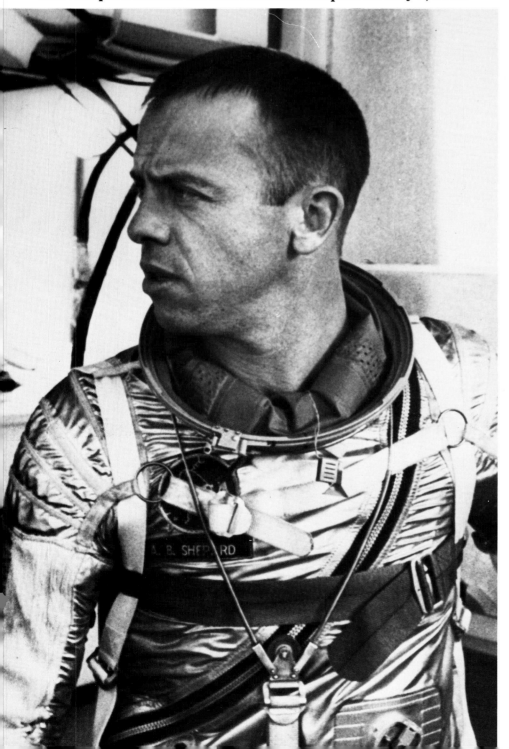

Alan Shepard became the first American in space on May 6, 1961.

An Atlas rocket carrying astronaut John Glenn roars into space on February 20, 1962.

The Space Program at Midpoint: Triumph and Tragedy

The Soviet Union continued to lead the space race through the mid-1960s. But America's space program was making steady gains. And NASA was working on a new program. It was called the Gemini series.

Gemini expanded on Mercury. Whereas the Mercury capsule could only hold one man, Gemini could hold two. NASA first launched two unmanned Gemini capsules. Then, on March 23, 1965, the first manned Gemini flight was made. Virgil Grissom went into space for the second time. He and his partner John Young made three orbits before returning to earth. While in flight, they used the new orbital maneuvering system. It was the first time a spacecraft had the ability to change orbits. Before this, other astronauts hadn't been able to control their crafts from space.

The next step was important in going to the moon. Systems for joining two separate crafts in space had to be developed. But NASA was not able to link up any Gemini crafts until the sixth and seventh flights. But the flight of Gemini 4 was notable for another reason.

One of the two Gemini 4 astronauts, Edward I. White, became the first American to "walk" in space. White left his spacecraft for 21 minutes during its third orbit around the earth. White actually floated in space while being secured to the spacecraft by a 25-foot long "double cord" line.

White's spacewalk duplicated a feat accomplished three months earlier by Soviet cosmonaut A. A. Leonov. Once again the United States was making advances in space. But once again NASA seemed to be just a step behind the Soviet Union.

After Gemini flights 6 and 7 made a successful space rendezvous, there were four more flights in the Gemini program. Eventually, two Gemini flights not only linked up, but were actually locked together.

NASA was very pleased at the conclusion of the Gemini program. Things were looking good for the American space effort. But these triumphs were soon followed by a stunning setback—and a disaster.

Tragedy on the Ground

Astronaut Gus Grissom had already had one brush with disaster. In July 1961, he had splashed down in the Atlantic Ocean after piloting the second American manned flight. His capsule rode the ocean swells while he waited to be rescued. Ships and helicopters were on their way. Grissom was supposed to open the hatch after they came. Then his rescuers would take him to an aircraft carrier.

There was a switch that opened

In 1965 astronaut Ed White walked in space. He was the first American to leave his spacecraft while in orbit. Tied to his Gemini 4 space capsule by a double cord, he spent 21 minutes outside the craft.

The Gemini 7 space capsule is photographed through the hatch window of Gemini 6 in December 1965. The two spacecraft ran through rendezvous maneuvers at an altitude of 160 miles.

the hatch. The switch was supposed to blow the bolts that kept the hatch closed. But the hatch didn't work right. The bolts blew off by themselves. Grissom didn't have a chance to use the switch. The problem was that the rescuers weren't there yet. The open space capsule started to fill with water. Grissom knew it was going to sink—he had to get out. Grissom barely escaped and the capsule was lost.

NASA fixed the hatch so that mistake couldn't happen again. The new hatch was much harder to open. It took more than 90 seconds to open it.

In January 1967, NASA was running more tests on Apollo 1, the first spacecraft in the moon program. The craft was built to hold three astronauts. One of them was Grissom. The other two were Edward White and Roger Chaffee.

The spacecraft wasn't ready for launch yet. On January 27 the three astronauts were in the capsule during a countdown rehearsal. And they were breathing pure oxygen.

Then a tiny spark set the oxygen on fire. The people working outside saw a burst of flame. And they saw hands inside the spacecraft trying to open the hatch. But it wouldn't open.

Tragically the hatch couldn't be opened from the outside either. The fire was too hot. Rescuers had to let it cool. It took six minutes. By then, all three astronauts were dead.

NASA scientists studied the fire. They found out that the spark came from some faulty wiring under Grissom's seat. And the fire was fueled by all the plastic in the capsule.

The fire went out when it ran out of air. But that filled the capsule with gases from the burning plastic. The astronauts were suffocated. It was a cruel irony. The improvements in the hatch that Grissom had asked for had cost him his life.

The disaster forced NASA to make many changes in the Apollo—about 5,000 all together. It took a long time.

There were no more manned flights for more than a year and a half. The next manned launch was Apollo 7 in October 1968.

NASA had been running the space program for nearly ten years. In all that time it had never lost an astronaut in space. Its only disaster happened on the ground. ∎

All three members of the flight crew died in the disastrous Apollo fire. The intense heat melted the large piece of plastic shown here. A stark symbol of the tragedy, the melted plastic covers up the American flag painted on the side of the craft.

Astronaut Edwin Aldrin becomes the second man to set foot on the surface of the moon. Fellow astronaut Neil Armstrong took this picture of his colleague.

Man on the Moon: The Longest Journey

The journey to the moon was a long one. It was filled with difficulties and disappointments. Each step, from Mercury 1 to Apollo 11, had a specific purpose. The challenges were many. A bigger rocket had to be built. And the astronauts needed to learn to navigate in space. The life-support system had to be perfect. Without it, the astronauts would die in space. And the astronauts needed to know where they would land. So they had to learn more about the moon.

The lunar lander had to work perfectly the first time. It couldn't be tested on earth. The rockets that

NASA had been using were not good enough. They could launch the Mercury and Gemini capsules into orbit around the earth, but they were not powerful enough for a moon shot.

Wernher von Braun built the rocket that NASA needed. It was called the Saturn V. It was used for the first time in November 1967 to launch Apollo 4.

Next, NASA had to send unmanned probes to the moon. These were called the Ranger series. The Ranger probes took thousands of pictures of the moon. NASA looked at all the pictures. And it finally

chose an area called the Sea of Tranquility as a landing site.

Still, many people were afraid that the moon's surface was soft. They worried that a spacecraft might sink into quicksand. So NASA had to find out how hard the surface of the moon was. Surveyor 1 was built to get that information.

When Surveyor 1 landed on the moon it took pictures of itself. The pictures showed that the craft didn't sink into the dust. Everyone was relieved; the surface was hard enough.

There were other problems to solve. NASA had to build a lunar lander. After separating from the spacecraft, this device would bring two of the astronauts down to a gentle landing on the moon's surface. And it would also take them back to their space capsule.

Apollo 5 was launched in January 1968 to test an unmanned lunar lander. Then in December 1968, Apollo 8 circled but did not land on the moon. Frank Borman, James Lovell, and William Anders were the Apollo 8 astronauts. They were the first human beings to see the moon close up.

But NASA wanted to test the lunar lander again. So Tom Stafford, Eugene Cernan, and John Young went up in Apollo 10. They took the

> The Apollo 8 astronauts were the first human beings to get a close look at the moon.

lander close to the moon, hovering just a few miles above the surface. But they didn't land. That would be Apollo 11's job.

A "Giant Leap for Mankind"

Apollo 11 was launched on July 16, 1969. If successful, this craft would put the first men on the moon.

The Saturn V rocket worked perfectly. It left the earth's orbit right on schedule. Then the three astronauts headed toward the moon. On the way, they broadcast the first color television pictures from space. They orbited the moon once before they got ready to land. Then Astronauts Neil Armstrong and Edwin (Buzz) Aldrin climbed into the lunar lander. Michael Collins stayed in the Apollo 11 spacecraft.

Next, the lander separated from the spacecraft. The astronauts radioed NASA, "The Eagle has wings!" Now those on the ground knew everything was going well.

Armstrong and Aldrin piloted the lander toward the moon's surface. But an equipment problem forced it off course. Armstrong had to manually land the craft.

Then on July 20, 1969, at 4:17 P.M. EST, Apollo 11 touched down. The first men had reached the moon! Armstrong radioed NASA. He announced, "The Eagle has landed." NASA radioed back: "You got a bunch of guys about to turn blue. We're breathing again. Thanks a lot."

Armstrong had to be careful. It was hard climbing down the ladder of the lander in his bulky spacesuit, while carrying a television camera. But millions of people around the world watched as another camera, attached to the lander, filmed him stepping onto the moon's surface.

Once more he radioed earth. This time the people of the world heard him say, "That's one small step for man, one giant leap for mankind."

Those eleven simple words summed up the feelings of millions of people back on earth—more than 243,000 miles from where Armstrong stood. ∎

The New York Times carried pictures of the first lunar landing. The images may have been fuzzy, but the subject matter was spectacular.

A '60s Olympic Scrapbook

ROME 1960: It had been a long hard road to the Olympics for **Wilma Rudolph.** A childhood illness had left her nearly crippled. She spent years recovering her strength. Then as a teenager, she showed great promise as a track star, first in high school, then later in college.

Wilma was a member of the U.S. Olympic team in 1956. But she did not fare well. She went back home and trained very hard for four years. In 1960 she was again a member of the U.S. team. This time the story was very different. She won gold medals in both the 100- and 200-meter dashes. Then as the anchor member of the 400-meter relay team, she earned another gold medal. She became the first American woman to win three Olympic gold medals.

ROME 1960: **Rafer Johnson** and **C. K. Yang** staged the greatest two-man duel in Olympic decathlon history. The 1500-meter race—the final event—decided the winner. Yang had beaten Johnson in each of the previous track events. But the stronger Johnson had won the field events by many points.

Now Yang had to beat Johnson in the 1500-meter race by several seconds in order to get more total decathlon points than his opponent. Around the track they ran. Johnson stayed on Yang's heels for the entire race. When they crossed the finish line Yang was in front—but only by four yards. The determined Johnson was the new decathlon champion.

MEXICO CITY 1968: The crowd, the judges, and even **Bob Beamon** himself, were stunned. Beamon had just competed in the long-jump event. When he landed at the end of the pit, he had gone beyond the range of the special measuring device. The judges had to measure his jump with a tape. Then they shook their heads in disbelief. When the result was announced, the entire stadium crowd gasped.

Beamon had jumped an incredible 29 feet, 2½ inches. He had broken the previous Olympic record by more than 2½ feet! In an event where previous records had been broken by only inches, Beamon's feat was almost impossible to believe.

Later, Beamon was asked to comment on how he had achieved such an accomplishment. "I was just lucky and everything fell together," he said.

INNSBRUCK 1964: When **Lidia Skoblikova** arrived at the 1964 Winter Games she was already a world class athlete. Four years before, she had won gold medals in the 1500-meter and 3000-meter speed skating races. And she was the current world record holder in the 500-meter and 1500-meter races.

Still, in 1964 Skoblikova stunned the Olympic world with her performances. She won gold medals in *four* speed skating events: the 500-meter, 1000-meter, 1500-meter, and 3000-meter races. And she set new Olympic records in three of the four events. Skoblikova became the first athlete ever to win four gold medals at the Winter Olympics.

Roger Maris Breaks a Cherished Record

All during the 1961 baseball season, a Yankee right fielder named Roger Maris chased a ghost. It was the ghost of another Yankee right fielder—Babe Ruth.

Maris was chasing one of baseball's most respected records—Ruth's single-season home run mark. In 1927 the great Bambino had hit 60 homers. Since then, no one had equaled that mark.

Entering the 1961 season, Maris was considered a fine outfielder and a good hitter. In 1960 he had won the American League's Most Valuable Player award. But he had never hit more than 39 homers in a season. He wasn't even the best home run hitter on his team. That honor went to slugger Mickey Mantle, a four-time home run champion.

But from the beginning of the '61 season, Maris began hitting home runs at a great pace. By the end of June he had 27. At the end of July, the total had reached 40. Mantle was also hitting homers at a great rate. His total at the end of July was 38.

By August, fans everywhere were talking about the "M & M" boys. Would Maris catch the Babe? Would Mantle? Would they both do it?

The battle continued throughout the hot days of August. On August 4, Maris hit his 41st homer. Two days later, Mantle hit his 41st, 42d, and 43d—in one game! The Yankees were battling for the pennant, but hardly anybody noticed. Everyone across the country was watching the M & M home run duel.

In mid-September Mantle hit his 54th home run. But Mantle had been battling injuries and an illness for weeks. Now his poor health was finally catching up with him. A week later he was forced out of the lineup for good. His challenge to Ruth was over.

That left only Maris. The pressure on him had become incredible. According to a ruling by Baseball Commissioner Ford Frick, Maris had to hit 60 or more homers in 154 games to beat Ruth's record. That was the same number of games Ruth had played in 1927. In 1961 baseball was playing a 162 game schedule. But Frick ruled that Maris's new mark wouldn't be considered the sole record if he needed the extra eight games to tie or break Ruth's total. Many people thought the ruling was unfair. But that was the way it was going to be.

News Across the Globe

Throughout the latter part of the season, newspaper and TV reporters followed Maris everywhere. Stories on his challenge to Ruth appeared as far away as Tokyo. It began to affect him, too. His hair fell out in big clumps. He had constant headaches and a bad case of the nervous shakes.

Through it all, he continued to hit home runs. On September 17, he hit his 58th. Four days later, in the Yankees 154th game, he hit his 59th—and no more. For some baseball fans, his chase was over. But for millions more, Maris still had eight games to set a new single-season home run record. Could he do it?

In game 158, Maris homered against Baltimore for his 60th of the year. He had tied the Babe.

Entering the final game, Maris still had 60. The Yankees were playing Boston at Yankee Stadium. The Boston pitcher was 24-year-old Tracy Stallard. In the fourth inning, Stallard threw Maris a fastball down the heart of the plate. Maris swung easily and the ball rocketed towards right field—and went in the stands!

The crowd stood and cheered for several minutes. Maris was mobbed at the Yankee dugout by his teammates. The chase was over. Baseball had a new single-season home run king. And his name was Roger Maris. ∎

Roger Maris connects for his record-breaking 61st homer.

Mr. Koufax—King of the Hill

When the 1960s began, Sandy Koufax was a struggling young pitcher with the Los Angeles Dodgers. Before the decade was half over, he was baseball's greatest pitcher. When he retired, some called him the greatest pitcher in baseball's history.

No pitcher has ever dominated baseball for a period of time the way Sandy Koufax did. For six years—1961–1966—he simply overwhelmed his opposition. Koufax had a blazing fastball and a dazzling curve ball. Sometimes he just blew the ball by a hitter. Other times he made them look silly when they swung at a curve and missed it by five feet.

Koufax was a very slow starter. As a young pitcher he could throw hard, but he had no control. When the hitters weren't hitting him hard, he was wild with his pitches. Entering the 1961 season he actually had a losing career record—36 wins, 40 losses.

Then suddenly in 1961, Koufax seemed to find himself. That year he won 18 games, and led the league in strikeouts with 269. In 1962 he was pitching very well again, when he became injured. He only pitched for about half a season but still won 14 games.

The next year Koufax really came into his own. He won 25 games, lost only 5, and had an incredible ERA of 1.88. In addition he struck out 306 batters. He led the league in wins, ERA, and strikeouts.

With Koufax leading the way, the Dodgers won the National League pennant in 1963. They faced their old New York rivals, the Yankees, in the World Series. Koufax started the first game. He struck out the first five hitters he faced and tied a World Series record. He went on to strike out 15 hitters that day to set a new Series record, and win the game 5–2.

Koufax beat the Yankees again in game 4, 2–1. That gave the Dodgers a clean four-game sweep and the championship.

Over the next three seasons Koufax was simply baseball's top pitcher. He won 19 games in 1964 (an injury once again cut short his season), 26 games in 1965, and 27 in 1966. His earned run averages were 1.74, 2.04, and 1.73. His strikeout totals were 223, 382 (a new single-season record), and 317.

In addition Koufax pitched a no-hitter in each of four straight seasons 1963–1966. That broke the record for career no-hitters held by the great Cy Young.

With Koufax as their pitching ace, the Dodgers won the pennant in 1965 and 1966. And they won the World Series in 1965 against the Minnesota Twins. Koufax won two more World Series games that year, including the deciding seventh game, 2–0.

At the end of the 1966 season, Koufax shocked the baseball world.

He announced his retirement. He was only 30, but his pitching arm was already suffering from arthritis. Doctors had warned him he could become permanently crippled if he continued to pitch.

All baseball fans and players were sad to see Sandy retire. In addition to his talent, he was a quiet, classy player who never spoke harshly about anyone. Opponents knew he would never try to embarrass them—even if he was beating them handily. For six short years, he had been king of the hill—the pitcher who people called Mr. Koufax. When he quit, many baseball people said there would never be another one like him. For all those who saw him pitch in his prime, it's hard to disagree with that view. ■

Sandy Koufax pitching in the first game of the 1963 World Series. Koufax struck out 15 Yankees to set a new Series record.

Joyous New York Mets fans mob the players after the final out of the 1969 Series against the Baltimore Orioles.

The Miracle Mets of '69

For years they had been the "joke" of baseball. Since the New York Mets entered the National League in 1962 they were baseball's biggest losers. In their first year they lost more games than any other team in history—120.

Throughout the sixties the Mets didn't improve very much. Each season they finished last, or next to last in the league. They couldn't hit well, couldn't pitch well, and their fielding . . . well, no one could bear to talk about that.

But despite their very poor play, the Mets had many, many fans. They played before large crowds at Shea Stadium. Some years they drew more than two million in attendance. Mets fans loved their team—but they always expected the worst.

In 1969, things seemed no different. The Mets had some good young pitchers, like Tom Seaver and Jerry Koosman. And they had a few

good hitters, like Tommie Agee and Cleon Jones. But they didn't seem to be going very far. By early August they trailed the first place Chicago Cubs by 9½ games.

Then, suddenly the Mets got hot—red hot. They played the Cubs several times during August and September and beat them easily. Before anyone realized what was happening, the Mets found themselves in first place! Mets fans—and most of baseball—couldn't believe it.

In mid-September the Mets clinched the Eastern Division title. Because baseball had a new division format, the Mets now had to play the Western Division Atlanta Braves for the National League pennant.

The Mets swept the Braves in three straight games. Their fans were in shock. The biggest losers in baseball up until 1969 were going to the World Series!

The cries of joy coming from

Mets rooters quickly stopped when they realized who the Mets would have to play in the Series. The American League champions were the Baltimore Orioles. All year the Orioles had steamrolled their American League opponents. Then they had clobbered the Minnesota Twins in the playoffs, sweeping three straight games. The "Big Bad Birds" were sure to bring the Mets back down to earth.

The Mets lost the first game of the Series. But then, they proved that 1969 was indeed a miracle year. They got fine pitching from Seaver and Koosman. And they got clutch hitting from Cleon Jones and Donn Clendennon, and some great fielding from Tommie Agee. The Mets won the next four straight to take the Series, 4–1. All of baseball was in shock . . . and New Yorkers went wild with joy. Baseball's biggest losers had become baseball's biggest winners. ∎

Two Giant Stars

Their battles on the "hard court" were classic. Pro basketball's greatest defensive player—Bill Russell—versus its greatest offensive star—Wilt Chamberlain. And they dominated their sport like no other players before them.

For 13 years Bill Russell was the heart and soul of the Boston Celtics. He led the Celtics to 11 championships in those 13 seasons. Five times he was the NBA's Most Valuable Player.

The 6-foot 9-inch Russell was never a great scorer. But no one ever blocked shots, grabbed rebounds, and defensively "clogged" the middle as well as he did.

Russell's defensive talents were always put to the strongest tests when he played against Chamberlain. At 7-feet 1-inch, Wilt the Stilt was a scoring machine. In 1962 he scored 100 points in a game against New York. That season he scored 4,029 points for an incredible average of 50.4 points a game.

Russell's Celtics dominated pro basketball in the 1960s. They won seven championships in a row. But Chamberlain's Philadelphia 76ers ended the Celtic streak in 1967 and captured the NBA title.

Russell retired in 1969. Chamberlain was traded to the Los Angeles Lakers in 1968. At the end of the decade Chamberlain was still setting scoring records.

The debate had raged for years: Who was better, Russell or Chamberlain? The answer was simple: There was only one player who could give Bill Russell trouble: Wilt Chamberlain. And there was only one player capable of stopping Wilt Chamberlain: Bill Russell. Case closed. ■

Wilt Chamberlain tries to get past Bill Russell in a scene they repeated hundreds of times throughout the '60s.

A "Guaranteed" Upset

A few days before Super Bowl III, New York Jets quarterback Joe Namath was being interviewed. Someone asked if he was worried about the game. His team was a 17-point underdog to the Baltimore Colts. Did he really think the Jets could win?

Namath smiled and said, "We'll win. I guarantee it." The next day Namath's statement made the front of every sports page in America.

Hardly any pro football follower in 1969 would have agreed with Namath. The Colts were a powerful and dominating team. They had lost only once during the season. And they had trounced the Cleveland Browns 34–0 in the NFL Championship Game.

The Jets on the other hand were considered lucky just to be in the Super Bowl. They had a good team, but had barely beaten the Oakland Raiders for the AFL Championship. Most football people thought the Colts' great defense would easily stop the Jets.

Yet, on Super Sunday, the entire football world watched in amazement as Namath made good on his guarantee. Using Namath's pinpoint passing and a ground-it-out running attack, the Jets scored 16 points. And the Jets' defense held the Colts' offense to only one touchdown. Final score: Jets, 16; Colts, 7.

Fans called it the biggest upset in pro football history. Joe Namath called it a guarantee he lived up to. ■

Quarterback Joe Namath hands the ball to running back Emerson Boozer during the Jets' great upset of the Colts in Super Bowl III.

The Supremes, Motown's most successful recording group.

The Sounds of the Sixties Were Blowin' in the Wind

Rock 'n' roll first got its name in the mid-1950s. Those words seemed to be the best way to describe the rhythm. The beat was hard-driving and alive. It made young people want to dance!

But adults didn't like rock 'n' roll music. They thought it was loud. (Usually it was.) Many parents even told their children that listening to rock 'n' roll would make them deaf. And most adults didn't like it because they thought it was earthy and sexual—and just not proper. Many teenagers would be the first ones to say that was true—that's why they loved it!

Many parents believed that rock 'n' roll was a fad craze of the '50s. They said it would pass—just like many other '50s fads. But they couldn't have been more wrong!

By the early '60s rock 'n' roll hadn't disappeared, it had only changed its sound a bit. The music became softer, more innocent. The hard-driving rhythms of Elvis Presley, Chuck Berry, and Little Richard had been replaced.

The new popular rock 'n' roll artists were people like Frankie Avalon and Fabian, and groups like the Four Seasons and the Beach Boys. The music was about love, dancing, good times, and America's latest recreational fad—surfing.

The "softer" music lasted only a few years. Unknown to many American teenagers, the rock 'n' roll of the fifties had had a powerful effect on teenagers elsewhere—especially in Great Britain.

A "British Invasion"

Elvis, Chuck Berry, and Buddy Holly had become very popular in England. And while American teenagers were "Surfin' USA" in the early '60s, British teens were listening to a whole new sound. It was created by musicians who had studied every swivel of Elvis's hips and every chord Berry and Holly had played. In 1964 this music hit the USA—and rock 'n' roll was never the same again.

The "British invasion" was led, of course, by the Beatles (see story on page 60). But they were just the tip of the iceberg. By the mid-1960s dozens of British groups were regularly climbing the American music charts. The Rolling Stones, The Who, The Animals, The Kinks, Jerry and the Pacemakers, and The Dave Clark Five were just a few of the many popular British groups of the '60s.

Their music returned rock 'n' roll to its '50s roots. The sound was hard-driving, rhythm-and-blues based, sometimes angry, often sexy. Before long American rock 'n' roll groups would start to copy that sound and another phase of American rock 'n' roll would begin.

At the same time the British invasion was occurring, American rock 'n' roll did produce one unique sound. It was called Motown. And it was pure silk and polish.

The "Motown Sound" was named after the Motown record company, started in Detroit by a man named Berry Gordy. It was the only record company that was able to create its own musical identity. The company only produced records by black artists. And many of them were heavily influenced by gospel music.

The Motown Sound usually consisted of strong rhythms, simple melodies, and perfect harmonies.

One Motown performer was Smokey Robinson. Along with his group, the Miracles, he had several big hits. Robinson also wrote songs for many other Motown artists.

Two other major all-male Motown groups were the Four Tops and the Temptations. They added another dimension to their live performances—dance routines performed as a background to their singing. They had several smash hits during the '60s.

The most successful Motown act, however, didn't dance and had no male singers. The group was the Supremes—three young women who had grown up together in Detroit, where Motown originated. The Supremes' smooth sound produced 12 number one hits in five years.

Songs of Protest

The Supremes—and the rest of Motown's artists—produced upbeat, noncontroversial songs. But at this time, an entirely different kind of music that *was* controversial was becoming popular. The folk rock music movement was filled with protest songs and artists who were concerned with society's problems. Without question, the leading voice of this music was Bob Dylan.

In 1962, the popular folk group, Peter, Paul, and Mary recorded a Dylan song called "Blowin' in the Wind." It talked about civil rights issues. It talked about war. And it made Bob Dylan famous.

As Dylan's popularity grew, his music changed. Dylan combined his folk songs with the rhythms of rock 'n' roll, thus creating the folk rock sound.

By the late 1960s rock 'n' roll had become rock music. And the widespread use of drugs by young people had given rise to psychedelic or "acid" rock.

The sounds of acid rock were hollow. They echoed, as if they had come from far away. And they haunted the listener with strange images.

Even the names of the acid rock groups were unusual. Like their music, their names were sometimes difficult to understand: Jefferson Airplane, Grateful Dead, Iron Butterfly, Moby Grape, and Buffalo Springfield.

Eventually, the antiwar movement helped merge folk rock with acid rock. This musical blend reached its peak in August 1969 at the Woodstock music festival.

Woodstock was unlike any other musical event. Nearly 500,000 people traveled to a small farm in New York. They went to hear three days worth of almost nonstop music. Nearly every top rock and folk rock group of the day was there.

At the end of the sixties, rock and roll was already 15 years old. It was still growing and still changing. And it was far from a fad. It was here to stay. ■

Bob Dylan, the leading voice of the folk rock movement during the '60s.

In August 1969, nearly 500,000 people flocked to the Aquarian rock festival in Woodstock, New York.

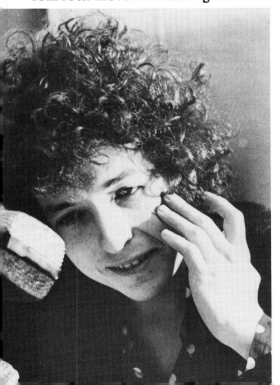

Beatlemania Hits America

In February 1964, a popular rising English rock 'n' roll group, named the Beatles, landed in America. Their presence was felt immediately. American teenagers went wild—especially teenage girls.

Everywhere the Beatles went, they were mobbed by adoring teenagers. Their fans screamed so much they weren't able to hear the group's music during their concerts. The fans' enthusiasm became so great that the press began to call it "Beatlemania."

Who were these four "mop-topped" musicians from England? The group was made up of four young men from a working class neighborhood in Liverpool. Their names were Paul McCartney, John Lennon, George Harrison, and Ringo Starr. McCartney, Lennon, and Harrison played guitar and Starr played drums.

The Beatles' songs, for the most part, were simple. Many of them were songs about love, as were most popular rock 'n' roll songs. The group's melodies, however, were unforgettable. And their harmonies were perfect. In any case, with their mop-top hairstyle and clean-cut look, the Beatles were what excited teenagers. No one since Elvis Presley had become so popular.

Throughout the mid-1960s the Beatles had one hit record after another. "I Want to Hold Your Hand," "She Loves You," "Please Please Me," "Love Me Do," "P.S. I Love You," "Hard Days Night," "Ticket to Ride," "Help!" the list went on and on. At one point in 1964, the group had the first five positions on the "top 40" rock 'n' roll music charts across the country.

As the decade progressed, the Beatles began to write songs about things other than love. They wrote about religion, drugs, and politics. But no matter what they wrote or sang, somehow the Beatles' music always touched their listeners personally.

In 1967 they produced their most impressive album, "Sgt. Pepper's Lonely Hearts Club Band." It contained music that was quite different from other Beatles' albums.

The group was accompanied by several studio musicians playing symphonic instruments. The stereo effect of the recordings was beyond any previous rock 'n' roll album. The songs themselves ranged from playful tunes such as "Lovely Rita, Meter Maid," and "When I'm Sixty-Four," to serious and thoughtful songs such as "She's Leaving Home," and "A Day in the Life."

By the late 1960s, it was becoming very difficult for the Beatles to perform in public. They were tired of always being mobbed. And it was hard for them to perform some of their songs outside the studio. There were certain sounds they just couldn't make on stage.

The Beatles stopped performing live in 1966. For the remainder of the decade, however, they continued to turn out interesting and more complex studio albums. By the end of the '60s, "Beatlemania" had just about disappeared. But the impact of the "fab four" on rock 'n' roll music—and society as a whole—would linger for a long, long time. ■

The Beatles, performing before a live audience at New York's Shea Stadium.

Robert Frost reciting a poem at President Kennedy's inauguration in January 1961.

Robert Frost— America's Poet

Although his back was bent, the tall white-haired man stood with dignity. It was bitterly cold on January 20, 1961. President-elect John F. Kennedy was about to be inaugurated. The old man was there for the ceremony. The wind whipped his hair and the paper he held. Finally, the old man stuck the paper in his pocket. From memory, he recited his poem, "The Gift Outright."

"The land was ours before we were the land's," he began. When he finished the poem, the crowd applauded wildly. They were cheering both the poem and the poet. At 86 years old, Robert Frost was an American legend.

Frost was born in San Francisco in 1874. When he was 11, his father died, and his family moved to Massachusetts. Frost attended high school there. Later he studied at Dartmouth and Harvard colleges, without getting a degree.

During that time he married Elinor White and started raising a family. To support them, Frost became a chicken farmer in New Hampshire. He also taught English and worked as an editor. But whenever he could find time, he wrote poetry.

When Frost was 38, he took his family to England. There, his first two books of poetry were published— *A Boy's Will*, and *North of Boston*. His poems were inspired by his experience in the farm country of New England. Both books were published in America in 1915. That same year, Frost and his family returned to New England.

Still, he wasn't earning much money from his poems. So he began to teach again and also to farm in the summer.

His poems were usually based on his life in the country. He wrote that poems should "begin in delight and end in wisdom."

Some of his poetry rhymed. Other poems followed a strict pattern but did not rhyme. Frost was a master of this technique of blank verse. Often his poems took the form of simple farm people talking.

He knew much unhappiness in his life. He was poor for a long time. Two of his six children died in infancy. Another died after she gave birth. Another committed suicide and a fifth suffered from mental illness. Frost's poems show the pain he felt. One poem is called "Home Burial." It centers around the tragedy of a child's death. Another poem, "The Hill Wife," shows a lonely woman living in the country. Her loneliness slowly drives her insane.

Despite Frost's painful life, he continued to write. In his lifetime he won four Pulitzer Prizes and other awards for his poetry.

When Frost died in 1963, President Kennedy echoed Frost's poem "Stopping by Woods on a Snowy Evening." Kennedy said, "He had promises to keep and miles to go, and now he sleeps." ■

Martin Luther King, Jr. Free at Last

On August 28, 1963, the streets of America's capital were packed. Some 200,000 marchers had come to Washington, D.C., to support civil rights. The man behind the demonstration was a black preacher from Alabama named Martin Luther King, Jr. That day he spoke to the huge crowd about his dream of equality for all Americans.

Millions would come to share that dream. King himself would die for it.

The Reverend Martin Luther King, Jr., was born in Atlanta, Georgia, in 1929. He was the son of a Baptist minister. An especially gifted student, King graduated from Morehouse College at the age of 19. He then earned a bachelor of divinity degree at Crozer Theological Seminary. In 1955 he earned his Ph.D. from Boston University.

That same year he came to national attention. He was then pastor of a Baptist Church in Montgomery, Alabama. To bring about integration, King was one of the organizers of a boycott of the Montgomery bus system.

He followed Indian leader Mahatma Gandhi's theory of peaceful resistance. King combined Christian thought with Gandhi's theory. He told his supporters, "We will not resort to violence. We will not degrade ourselves with hatred. Love will be returned for hate."

In 1957 he organized the Southern Christian Leadership Conference (SCLC). Now he was more than a Baptist minister from a single church. He spoke for a large group of people.

For the next several years he led sit-ins and protest marches all over the South. He was often arrested and jailed.

In 1964 he won the Nobel Peace Prize for bringing change through peaceful means. At 35, he was the youngest person ever so honored.

In 1965 he led a voter-registration march in Selma, Alabama. His people were attacked, and some were killed. Across the nation, people spoke out in support of King's cause.

The courageous, nonviolent protest had an effect. Partly because of it, the Voting Rights Act of 1965 was passed.

By 1968 King was active in the antiwar movement. He saw the Vietnam War as a drain on America's resources. It was using money that could help poor blacks survive. Also, some felt that an unfairly large number of blacks fought and died in Vietnam.

King was preparing to lead a "Poor People's Campaign" when tragedy struck. On April 4, 1968, King was shot and killed in Memphis, Tennessee. A white man, James Earl Ray, was found guilty of the murder. He was sentenced to 99 years in prison.

Around the world, people mourned. King was buried in Atlanta. Above his grave were written words from an old slave song. They were words King had often recalled in his speeches.

"Free at last, Free at last, Thank God Almighty, I'm free at last." ∎

The Reverend Martin Luther King, Jr., (shown center with his wife Coretta) celebrates the successful 1956 bus boycott in Montgomery, Alabama.

A Powerful Voice for Change
Malcolm X

Not all American blacks were willing to follow Martin Luther King's policy of nonviolent resistance. Some black leaders, such as Malcolm X, believed that blacks would never be treated fairly or be granted equality by whites.

Malcolm X was the chief spokesman of the Black Muslim movement during the 1950s and early 1960s. The Black Muslim movement was started by W. D. Fard in the early 1930s in Detroit. Fard claimed to be an Arabian prophet. He taught a kind of religion he called Islam. "Reject Christianity," he urged his followers. "It is the white man's religion." He taught his followers to be proud of their heritage. And he promised that one day the blacks would overthrow the whites.

In 1934 the movement was taken over by Elijah Muhammad. Elijah had a deep hatred of whites, referring to them as "blue-eyed devils." He was not interested in the integration of blacks into white society. His goal, instead, was the creation of a separate black nation within the United States.

Over the years the Black Muslims bought large farms in several Southern states. There they grew food for their own restaurants and food stores. They also set up their own schools, churches, and businesses. They lived by a strict moral code. Drinking and smoking were forbidden. Many ex-convicts were welcomed into the group and were helped to become responsible citizens. One of these was Malcolm X.

Malcolm was born in Omaha, Nebraska, in 1925. His real name was Malcolm Little. When he became a Black Muslim, he changed his name to "X" as a protest. His real name, he believed, was a slave's name. And he didn't want to be associated with slavery.

Malcolm had learned to hate whites early in life. When he was a child, his family's home was burned by the Ku Klux Klan. Then Malcolm's father was killed. The death appeared to have been an accident. But Malcolm always believed his father had been murdered by white racists.

In 1946 Malcolm was sentenced to prison in Massachusetts for burglary. While in prison, he learned about the Black Muslims. When he was released from prison in 1952, he joined the movement. Because he was a very dynamic and forceful speaker, he quickly gained popularity. Soon he had become the Muslims' leading spokesman.

By the beginning of the 1960s Malcolm X became one of the most controversial men in the United States. He spoke throughout the nation and in Africa, Europe, and the Middle East. He appeared on radio and television programs, and spoke at colleges and universities. He was very popular among blacks. He was able to express in words, clearly and forcefully, what many blacks felt but were unable to say.

By 1963 Malcolm's views were changing. He left the Black Muslims and formed his own group, the Organization for Afro-American Unity. By 1965 Malcolm's racial views had greatly changed. He had overcome much of his hatred for whites. He now believed that blacks and whites should work together to build a more democratic and just society.

On February 21, 1965, Malcolm X was giving a speech at the Audubon Ballroom in New York City. Suddenly three men charged at him firing weapons. Malcolm went down.

Sixteen bullets had entered his body. The three killers were caught. Two of them were Black Muslims.

Malcolm's followers saw his death as a sacrifice for the "black revolution." Most blacks were shocked and saddened by the assassination. And today, Malcolm X is considered a hero by many black Americans. ■

Malcolm X, a leading Black Muslim spokesman, moderated his racial views during the 1960s.

OUR CENTURY: 1960-1970

GLOSSARY

acid: a slang term for the hallucinogenic drug, LSD. The experience of taking the drug was called an "acid trip."

antiwar movement: protest activities and demonstrations that expressed many Americans' belief that the country should not be involved in the war in Vietnam.

Berlin Wall: a barrier erected in 1961 to divide the city of Berlin, Germany, in two, with one side part of the Federal Republic of Germany, and the other part of the Communist German Democratic Republic.

boycott: an organized refusal to use certain services or buy certain goods as a way of registering protest.

British Invasion: the term used for the influx of popular British bands onto the American rock 'n' roll scene in the early 1960s.

doves: a term used for liberal, antiwar Americans during the Vietnam War.

freedom rides: rides organized to test laws that required different racial groups to use separate buses, or a separate section of a bus.

hawks: a term used for conservative, pro-war Americans during the Vietnam War.

hippie: a term used in the 1960s to refer to a person who dressed unconventionally and rejected many aspects of traditional society.

mini-skirts: very short skirts that were fashionable during the early 1960s.

Motown: a slang term for Detroit, the "Motor City."

nonviolence: a method of protesting injustice that stresses the use of peaceful, or nonviolent, strategies.

offensive weapons: weapons designed to use in attacks against another nation.

Peace Corps: a program organized by President Kennedy that sent young Americans overseas to lend a hand in developing countries.

segregation: the practice of forcing people of different racial backgrounds to be apart in every sort of activity.

Tet: Vietnam's celebration of the lunar new year, and the country's most important holiday.

Vietcong: guerilla fighters during the Vietnam War who opposed the South Vietnamese government.

BOOKS FOR FURTHER READING

The titles listed below provide more detailed information about some of the people and events described in this book. Ask for them at your local library or bookstore.

Daring the Unknown: A History of N.A.S.A. Smith (Harcourt Brace Jovanovich)

The Incredible Sixties. The Stormy Years That Changed America. Archer (Jules' Books)

John F. Kennedy. Graves (Dell)

Renaissance of Rock. Sounds of America: The Sixties. Kallen (Abdo & Daughters)

Rock. An Illustrated History. Barnard (Schirmer Books)

We Shall Overcome: Heroes of the Civil Rights Movement. Powledge (Macmillan Children's Group)

PLACES TO WRITE OR VISIT

Communications Hall of Fame
72 Mountain Street
Sutton, Quebec J0E 2K0

John F. Kennedy Presidential Library
& Museum
Columbia Point
Boston, MA 02125

National Afro-American Museum &
Cultural Center
1350 Brush Row Road
P.O. Box 578
Wilberforce, OH 45384

INDEX